Live Lent!

Year C

By Sr. Theresa Rickard, O.P.

Weekday reflections by Deacon Charles Paolino

RENEW International gratefully acknowledges the contributions to this work by Martin A. Lang.

NIHIL OBSTAT
    Rev. Christopher M. Ciccarino, S.S.L., S.T.D.

IMPRIMATUR
    Joseph W. Cardinal Tobin, C.Ss.R.
    Archbishop of Newark

Cover design by Ruth Markworth
Interior Design Consultant: Blue Willow Publishing Works
Interior Page Layout by Clara Baumann
Cover photo © Radu Razvan Gheorghe | Dreamstime.com

ISBN: 978-16203-144-7

RENEW International
    1232 George Street
    Plainfield, NJ 07062-1717
    www.renewintl.org

Printed and bound in the United States of America

Contents

LIVE LENT!

Theresa Rickard, O.P.

My annual retreat is often at St. Mary's Retreat Center in Cape May, New Jersey. One September, I experienced an additional blessing—thousands of monarch butterflies in the skies of Cape May, stopping for a few weeks on their way to Mexico. During the retreat, we were encouraged to attend a presentation at Cape May Point State Park about the monarch phenomenon. The Cape May Bird Observatory is a leader in monarch butterfly migration research; observatory staff study and tag butterflies during their southward migration. Monarchs tagged in Cape May have been found at numerous locations farther south, even at their final destination in Mexico. The butterfly and the transformation they undergo and their incredible migration were part of a key reflection for me during my retreat. I love the remark by Archbishop Desmond Tutu, *"God does not look at the caterpillar we are now, but the dazzling butterfly we have in us to become."*

A caterpillar, which can only crawl, seems to have limited potential. But as it grows, it renews itself over and over by growing a new skin while shedding the old one that can no longer contain it. When it has shed the last confining skin, the caterpillar seems to disappear within a fragile shell but re-emerges in a glorious new life marked by color and flight. From its beginning as a tiny egg, the caterpillar is destined to that new life; everything it does moves it closer to the day when it will spread those colorful wings and, to paraphrase an aviator, slip the bonds of earth and touch the face of God.

Bishop Tutu picked the transformation of a caterpillar into a butterfly as an analogy for the transformation to which God has called each one of us. Our response to that call is at the heart of the season of Lent. During Lent, the Church encourages us to devote time and attention to the process of conversion in our lives, the process of becoming our best and truest selves, the process of growing beyond the worldly things that burden us, and taking flight in the freedom that comes only through friendship with God.

This conversion does not happen on one day or during one season of Lent. Although we have moments of insight or elation—and although we may have setbacks—conversion is for most of us a step-by-step movement forward. The goal of this gradual progress is what philosophers such as the Jesuit Bernard Lonergan have called "self-transcendence," an ability to see the world as bigger than ourselves. This doesn't mean that we are insignificant in that bigger world; it means that each of us has an indispensable part to play outside of our own pleasures, interests, and concerns.

In other words, "self-transcendence" is the opposite of self-absorption, the opposite of going through life thinking only of ourselves, of our own security and convenience and comfort. Although self-absorption is an expression of selfishness, a self-absorbed person isn't necessarily malicious. On the contrary, a self-absorbed person is just as likely to simply be stuck in place, used to a certain safe routine designed to avoid risk—perhaps the risk of opening the heart to other people and particularly to people in material or spiritual need; to people who are "different" because of their race, ethnicity, religion, or sexual orientation.

That's where Lent comes in. Lent is an invitation for us Christians to ask ourselves if we are stuck in place. As we think about this question, we have a model in Jesus himself whose life was defined by generosity and self-sacrifice, by unconditional love. We become authentic human beings, the human beings God intended us to be, when we imitate that love. Lent is a time to pause and consider how far we have moved toward that ideal, to ask what may stand in our way, and to commit ourselves to taking even modest steps forward.

This year we once again strive to *Live Lent!* with the resolve to make real change in our lives—to become the dazzling butterfly we have in us to become.

Preparing for Lent

For me, the Lenten season has always been a time to refocus on God and get my life in right order. I want to Live Lent! so I can live faith with greater integrity and in deeper communion with God and my neighbor.

I have come to realize that Lent is not so much about giving up things as it is about seizing the opportunity to be all that God has called me to be—a holy, healthy, and loving person—a disciple of Jesus Christ committed to transforming my faith into real-life action.

So, let me suggest not ways to fast but things to do and things not to do this Lent. First, things to do:

Consciously surrender to God. Whenever we say the Lord's Prayer we ask that God's will be done on earth. And Lent reminds us that leading a Christian life means setting aside our will—our desires and wishes and priorities—and asking God to help us behave only according to his will.

Let go of old self-images. Imitating Jesus, who died on the cross, is to empty ourselves of ego and see ourselves as who we really are—creatures totally dependent on our Creator, but also living reflections of God's love and compassion. We are flawed and fabulous, and we need to let go of denigrating ourselves and old tapes that tell us that we are not good enough or smart enough or attractive enough. Lent is a time to see ourselves clearly—as Father Richard Rohr's says, to find our true selves, our God selves, our Christ selves.

Focus on engendering life from within. No matter what we own or what we lack in the way of material possessions or wealth, our greatest gifts to each other, to the world at large, will always come from within us. Be conscious of the Holy Spirit encouraging your powers of love, compassion, and justice; realize the potential in these gifts; find ways to use these gifts to bless the lives of others in large ways and small.

Ask for the grace of transformation. Pray each day that you will emerge from this Lenten experience as a new person. Leave the details of your renewal up to God, and thank God for this grace.

And now, things not to do:

Don't give up. Instead of giving up something for Lent, try doing something that will bring you closer to God. Perhaps attend Mass during the week, spend time reflecting on the daily or Sunday readings by yourself and with others by using this book, experience the beauty of God's creation by taking walks, make donations to your favorite charities, volunteer at the local food bank, light candles and say prayers for the people you know who are struggling. If you still decide to give something up, do it for someone else. For example, if you give up wine for Lent, each time you decline to take wine, pray for someone who struggles with an addiction to alcohol.

Don't sweat it. Whatever it is you commit to do this Lent, the point isn't to do it perfectly. Give it your best, but if you slip up, accept that as a reminder that you are not perfect. Only God is perfect. Say a prayer, and start again.

Don't starve yourself. Lent isn't about going on a diet or losing weight—it's about the conversion of hearts. Eat healthy, get some exercise, but don't succumb to our culture's obsession with physical appearances. Again, if you want to give up sweets, do it while praying for someone who is seriously overweight.

Don't make it more difficult than it is. The three pillars of Lent are prayer, fasting, and almsgiving. Find simple ways to pray, fast, and give to those who live in poverty.

Don't hold back. Lent will present you with many opportunities to convert your heart and your life, to heal broken relationships, and to grow closer to God. When you find yourself presented with such an opportunity, embrace it.

So this Lent don't give up, don't sweat it, don't starve yourself, don't make it more difficult than it is, and, most especially, don't hold back! Live Lent! so you can live a more authentic faith long after these 40 days have passed.

40 Days to Live Lent!

A good Lent begins with a plan. Just as we carefully plan for big events in our personal lives, such as a graduation or a wedding, Lent invites us to make our hearts ready for remembering Jesus' passion and celebrating Jesus' resurrection. The best way to celebrate Jesus' resurrection is to live more fully Christ's life in the here and now.

What are some actions this Lent that can deepen your relationship with God, make you more aware of God's presence in your life, and help you to be kinder, more loving, to others? Reflect on your life and where you are in your relationship with God. Which relationship in your life most needs forgiveness and God's healing presence? What are you doing for people who are living in poverty? What bad habit is keeping you away from God? What do you need to change? Pray about it; ask God. We can't make changes in our lives without God's grace. Willpower is never enough.

Now, write down simple actions under each of the three areas we are invited to act on during Lent: prayer, fasting, and almsgiving (giving to those in need and supporting our parish and other worthy organizations). Many parishes participate in CRS Rice Bowl program through which millions of Catholics in the United States apply the Lenten pillars of praying, fasting, and almsgiving to help alleviate hunger around the world. See if your parish does this, or help to establish the program in your parish. For more information, go to www.crsricebowl.org.

We are called to live Lent so we can live faith not only during these 40 days but every day henceforth.

Jot down the commitments you will make in each of these areas. Remember, keep it simple and doable. Review your Lenten commitments each Sunday during Lent and make adjustments. Don't give up; keep at it.

Prayer:

_____
_____
_____
_____
_____
_____
_____
_____

Fasting:

_____
_____
_____
_____
_____
_____
_____
_____

Almsgiving:

_____
_____
_____
_____
_____
_____
_____
_____

Ash Wednesday

 Pray

"Even now, says the Lord, return to me with your whole heart. . . ."
(Joel 2:12)

 Read *Matthew 6: 1-6, 16-18*

Summary: *"But when you pray, go to your inner room, close the door, and pray to your Father in secret. And your Father who sees in secret will repay you." (Matthew 6:6)*

Spend two minutes in silence. Then repeat this passage from Scripture, and let it speak to your heart.

 Meditation

When Lieutenant Colonel Tim Collins addressed troops of the Royal Irish Regiment as they prepared for war in Iraq in 2003, he told them, "I know of men who have taken life needlessly in other conflicts; I can assure you that they live with the mark of Cain upon them."

Col. Collins alluded to the mark that God put on Cain, son of Adam and Eve, after Cain killed his brother Abel.

According to the Book of Genesis, God cursed Cain, saying that the ground would no longer yield produce for Cain, who would live as a fugitive. But when Cain protested that someone might kill him, God put a mark on him as a sign that anyone who harmed him would be severely punished.

The Scripture says that Cain and his wife had a son, and that Cain built a city and named it after the boy.

The "mark of Cain" evokes punishment and guilt—as Col. Collins used the term—just as the ashes we are marked with today evoke penance and mortality.

Cain went on living, established a family, and—if building a city counts—was a productive member of society.

In a parallel way, we are encouraged to pause, as our heads are marked with ashes, to repent the ways we have offended God, and also resolve to live from now on in keeping with the Gospel.

Today is the beginning of Lent. It is also the beginning of looking forward to the resurrection of Jesus and to our own rising to new life.

Live Lent!

I will receive the sacrament of reconciliation. I will put the past behind me and begin anew.

 Pray

Lord Jesus, your life on earth was a model of humility. Help me to imitate you in that virtue, showing my devotion not through extravagant displays, but rather through quiet and heart-felt prayer. Amen.

Thursday after Ash Wednesday

 Pray

"Choose life, then, that you and your descendants may live, by loving the Lord, your God, heeding his voice, and holding fast to him." (Deuteronomy 30:19b-20a)

 Read *Luke 9:22-25*

Summary: *"What profit is there for one to gain the whole world yet lose or forfeit himself?"* (Luke: 9:25)

Spend two minutes in silence. Then repeat this passage from Scripture, and let it speak to your heart.

 Meditation

Education, when I was a student, involved a canon of American and

English literature including poems by such figures as Robert Frost and William Wordsworth.

I can recall only fragments of those poems, but there is one—by Edwin Arlington Robinson—that I have remembered since the first time I read it in high school. The poem was "Richard Cory," in which Robinson described a man who was universally admired for his manners, his appearance, and his wealth.

There's no hint that those who admired Richard Cory also resented him, but, the poet wrote, they thought Richard Cory was everything to make them wish that they were in his place. So, they continued with their hardscrabble lives, and Richard Cory, on a "calm summer night," shot himself to death.

That poem stuck with me, because it was such a blunt restatement of the lesson Jesus preached: What does it profit a man to gain the whole world if, in the bargain, he loses himself?

People in our culture are subject more than ever to messages encouraging them to acquire goods far beyond what they need to live decently and, if need be, go into debt to accomplish it. It is not coincidental that this pervasive atmosphere of consumerism has been accompanied by a decline in religious practice.

Richard Cory's neighbors may have struggled to make ends meet, but if they thought material wealth would guarantee a more fulfilling life, his fate should have taught them otherwise.

Lent is an invitation for us to reflect on the true sources of fulfillment—our relationship with God and with our fellow human beings. If those relationships are in order, we need envy no one.

Live Lent!

I will make a list of things I would like to acquire and then cross off the ones that would not improve my relationships with God and my fellow human beings.

 Pray

Lord Jesus, you lived with virtually no material possessions,

and yet you changed the world. Saints such as Francis of Assisi and Teresa of Calcutta have done the same. Help me to avoid attachment to things that do not matter and to devote myself instead to building up your kingdom on earth. Amen.

 Pray

"This … is the fasting that I wish…. Sharing your bread with the hungry, sheltering the oppressed and the homeless; Clothing the naked when you see them, and not turning your back on your own." *(Isaiah 58:6-7)*

 Read *Matthew 9:14-15*

Summary: "The days will come when the bridegroom is taken away from them, and then they will fast." *(Matthew 9:15)*

Spend two minutes in silence. Then repeat this passage from Scripture, and let it speak to your heart.

 **Meditation**

Ross Cochrane, an Australian minister, told about a wedding in which the groom arrived very late. The driver of the bride's limo was instructed to circle the block until the groom was at his post.

No doubt the family and friends were in a state of anticipation—and maybe a little worry—as the celebration was delayed. Did the groom lose the ring? Was he stuck in traffic? Did he change his mind? And no doubt the guests were relieved when the young man bustled in and took his place.

That period of anticipation, and worry, is an analogy for the period in which the world awaited its Savior. But when he came, those who recognized him had reason to celebrate as they entered, through him, into a new relationship with God and with all of humanity.

Jesus did introduce something new, a far more intimate connection with God than men and women had ever known. Those, such as John's disciples, who tried to fit this new reality into an old understanding, were missing the radical meaning of the birth and ministry of Jesus.

The Lord had come. That was cause for joy. And although, as Jesus foretold, his followers would mourn his death and wrestle with the implications of his ascension, they would rejoice again when they understood—and told anyone who would listen—that he would always be with them, in the Eucharist, in the Church, and in his Holy Spirit.

We pause during Lent to contemplate the suffering and death of Jesus and our own many deaths of sin or indifference, but we will emerge from Lent with confidence that the Bridegroom will be always at our side, in this life and in the life to come.

Live Lent!

I will write "I am with you" on a file card, and carry that card with me wherever I go. Whenever I see it, I will reflect on how my circumstances at that moment are transformed by my consciousness of Christ's presence.

 Pray

Lord Jesus, I am consoled by the promise you made to your disciples: "I am with you until the end of time." Help me live every hour, to make every decision, while conscious that you are by my side. Amen.

Saturday after Ash Wednesday

 Pray

"For you, O Lord, are good and forgiving, abounding in kindness to all who call upon you." (Psalm 86:15)

Read *Luke 5:27-32*

Summary: *"Jesus said to them in reply, 'Those who are healthy do not need a physician, but the sick do.'"* (Luke 5:31)

Spend two minutes in silence. Then repeat this passage from Scripture, and let it speak to your heart.

 **Meditation**

One of the most persistent scams that Americans are subject to is the "phone call from the Internal Revenue Service." The general theme of the call is that the recipient owes federal taxes, has to pay them now, and can do so by providing a debit or credit card number.

The IRS has responded to this fraud by reiterating that the agency never uses phone calls or email to notify folks of outstanding taxes, but enough people fall for it to make it worthwhile for the scammers to persist in preying on people's fear of the tax collector.

Using the tax code in order to cheat people is nothing new; in fact, it was rampant during the lifetime of Jesus. The Gospels give us two examples of men who themselves were tax collectors and who used the system to bilk people out of the cash or produce that were used to pay taxes in those days.

Getting a phone call from a phony IRS operative raises a question about the persons making such calls. Do they feel somehow justified in cheating others out of hard-earned money? Do their consciences bother them at all?

These same questions would have applied to Levi, whom we know better as the apostle Matthew, and to Zacchaeus, another dishonest tax collector, who appears in the nineteenth chapter of Luke's Gospel.

Levi and Zacchaeus both presumably went merrily on filching money from defenseless subjects of the Roman Empire and didn't lose sleep over it—until, that is, they encountered Jesus.

In both cases, these men took the Gospel to heart and changed their lives.

Most of us are not in need of so radical a conversion, but the kind of self-examination that seems to elude bogus IRS agents can help us to confront any aspects of our lives that may be keeping us from surrendering our wills completely to the will of God.

Lent is the perfect opportunity to undertake that inner search with confidence that God will accept our penance and forgive our mistakes.

Live Lent!

I will spend some time considering how my will has not been in keeping with God's will. I will pray a sincere Act of Contrition.

 Pray

Almighty God, you have made your will clear, proclaiming it in the Commandments and in the teaching of your Son, Jesus Christ. Help me to live thoughtfully, trying always to make my decisions and choices with your will as my guide and accepting my penitence when I do not. Amen.

First Sunday of Lent

Jesus is Tempted, Jesus is Freed

Suggested Environment

A small table with a burning candle and a Bible opened to the gospel reading for this session. Consider decorating the table with violet, the liturgical color of the Lenten season.

Liturgical Readings for the
First Sunday of Lent

DEUTERONOMY, 26:4-10
"…we cried to the LORD, the God of our fathers,
and he heard our cry
and saw our affliction, our toil, and our oppression.
He brought us out of Egypt
with his strong hand and outstretched arm…"

PSALM 91:1-2,10-11,12-13,14-15
"Be with me, Lord, when I am in trouble."

ROMANS 10:8-13
"For there is no distinction between Jew and Greek;
the same Lord is Lord of all,
enriching all who call upon him.
For *"everyone who calls on the name of the Lord will be saved."*

LUKE 4:1-13

*"Filled with the Holy Spirit, Jesus returned from the Jordan
and was led by the Spirit into the desert for forty days,
to be tempted by the devil."*

Focus

Examining the motivations behind our temptations and sins and bringing them to prayer help us to make better choices as we grow in our spiritual lives.

Opening Song (To download, visit ocp.org/renew-music.)

"Eagle's Wings," Michael Joncas

 Opening Prayer

Divide the group in two, and pray together from Psalm 91, with everyone repeating the response:

R. (cf. 15b) **Be with me, Lord, when I am in trouble.**

Side 1: *You who dwell in the shelter of the Most High,*
who abide in the shadow of the Almighty,
say to the LORD, "My refuge and fortress,
my God in whom I trust."

R. **Be with me, Lord, when I am in trouble.**

Side 2: *No evil shall befall you,*
nor shall affliction come near your tent,
for to his angels he has given command about you,
that they guard you in all your ways.

R. **Be with me, Lord, when I am in trouble.**

Side 1: *Upon their hands they shall bear you up,*
lest you dash your foot against a stone.
You shall tread upon the asp and the viper;
you shall trample down the lion and the dragon.

R. **Be with me, Lord, when I am in trouble.**

Side 2: *Because he clings to me, I will deliver him;*
I will set him on high because he acknowledges my name.
He shall call upon me, and I will answer him;
I will be with him in distress;
I will deliver him and glorify him.

R. **Be with me, Lord, when I am in trouble.**

All: **Amen.**

🔲 The Gospel of the Lord

Filled with the Holy Spirit, Jesus returned from the Jordan
and was led by the Spirit into the desert for forty days,
to be tempted by the devil.
He ate nothing during those days,
and when they were over he was hungry.
The devil said to him,
"If you are the Son of God,
command this stone to become bread."
Jesus answered him,
"It is written, One does not live on bread alone." (Luke 4:1-4)

Read aloud Luke 4:1-13

Reflect

What word, phrase, or image from the gospel reading touches your heart or connects to your experience? Share with the group, and/or write your response here:

_____

_____

_____

_____

Old Testament Connections

The temptations of Jesus in the Judean desert remind us of the warnings of Moses before his people entered the Promise Land. Temptation is a theme throughout the Old Testament. When the people were wandering in the desert after leaving the Sinai Peninsula, rabble rousers stirred them to complain about the God-given and hunger-satisfying bread, the manna from heaven (Nm 11:1-12). They wanted to abandon the leadership of Moses (and thus God) to re-submit themselves to the authority of the pagan pharaoh. In this way they would once again be able to eat fresh fish, cucumbers, onions, and melons.

This same theme was threaded through Israel's conduct when the people finally reached the Promised Land. They often sold out to the worship of fertility gods in hope of being blessed with abundant crops. The Canaanite gods, again and—not coincidently—golden bulls, appear to control all the production of food. People must worship the gods in order to have productive fields.

Later, the prophet Elijah would finally turn many away from this practice and establish God as the source of all fertility and thus the production of food. The Old Testament tradition preserves in song the memories of these temptations and sins not by criticizing Israel but by praising God, "for his mercy endures forever" (Ps 107). The Gospel of Luke catches the spirit of the psalmist by emphasizing the "God side" of temptation, that is God's forgiveness and mercy especially when we succumb to temptation.

The devil in our gospel scene is not different from the golden bulls of old, representing material prosperity and human control as the gods of false worship. This is the background of our text on the temptations of Jesus. Against this backdrop we see God's true Son, Jesus, as the new Israel, repeating the ancient words of God's teaching in a new key, in a new place, at a new time; temptation is overcome. With God's grace we, too, can resist temptation, and when we stumble we rely on God's forgiveness and mercy to lift us up and put us back on our spiritual journey—a journey that leads to healing and fullness of life.

Adapted from a reflection by Martin A. Lang in Luke: My Spirit Rejoices!, *part of the* RENEW Scripture Series.

Reflect

How does God respond to the unfaithfulness of the Israelites?

Identify some of the false gods we worship in our society.

Share with the group, or write your response here:

_____

_____

_____

_____

 Meditation

I find it comforting that Jesus was tempted but that he overcame his temptations. Temptations in themselves are not sinful, but they can lead us to sinful acts. Jesus did not give in to the three temptations presented to him—possessions, popularity, and power—yet he experienced them in all their intensity. "He was tempted in every way we are, yet never sinned" (Heb 4:15). We all experience temptations; it is part of our human condition. It is paradoxical that material things (and sometimes people) that attract us can sometimes lead to our degradation—the opposite of the purpose-filled life God desires for us. I am grateful we have a merciful God who gives us the grace to resist temptation and, when we can't resist, gives us another chance to become our best selves—free to love and be loved.

Jesus was tempted in the desert as he was about to begin his ministry, after he had been anointed by the Spirit in the River Jordan. Toward the end of his 40-day stint in the desert, Jesus was tired and hungry—for me, an ideal situation in which temptation might lure me in. Jesus experienced the depth of human need. Immediately, the devil came to him, offered him a quick and easy way out of the human condition. The devil urged him to be God—all powerful and eternal— but to reject his humanity. Jesus refused to be trapped by the evil one and left the desert tested, true, and free to take on his mission to save the world.

Lent is our time in the desert and becomes our battleground with the same human temptations. For me, the first step in resisting temptation is to recognize that I am being tempted, acknowledge it for what it is, and then ask for God's grace to choose the better way. Temptation leads to sin, and sin separates us from God and thus from becoming our true selves. Sin can trap us if we refuse to let it go.

I saw a metaphor for this challenge when I was giving a retreat in South Africa. The sister in charge of the kitchen was constantly chasing monkeys out with a broom, because they would sneak in to steal fruit.

She explained that the local planters have a way of catching the monkeys that raid the banana plantations. A planter splits a coconut in two, scoops out the insides and puts in something a monkey can't resist. The planter then seals up the coconut and makes a slit large enough for the monkey to slip its hand in. When a monkey places its hand inside the coconut and grasps the sweet, its fist is too big to pull back out. The monkey will pull and push in an effort to get that sweet out, but it will not let it go, not even as the captors approach. The monkey is dimly aware that if it doesn't let go it will be captured. But the monkey can't free itself from its desire to possess its newfound treat and so is trapped.

Often in life we are like the monkey, presented with what seems like an irresistible offer, yet dimly aware that unless we let it go it will trap us. But we still hang on even if it is hurting us and our loved ones. In my own life, the little and most unconscious things trap me. During my last annual retreat, eight days of silence and prayer—a desert experience for me—I struggled with why I overcommit myself. When I am at my most compulsive, there is little time left between events for silence and space. I then find myself literally struggling to breathe. I know that is not God's will for me. I get lots of affirmation for my overactivity—that's the sweet in the coconut. I like being a superwoman. However, when I cross the line and take on one thing too many, I become anxious and I lose a sense of freedom and joy. Often, when I become over-extended, I become cranky and resentful— so much for being a superwoman for God. I have tried to resist this compulsion of overactivity, and often it works for a few months, and then I am back to my old ways.

At this last retreat, my spiritual director invited me to look at the motivations behind my over-commitment. One of the biggest impediments to spiritual growth is that we do not perceive our hidden motivations. I prayed and asked God to purify my motivations. This led me to discover that much of my desire to achieve comes from wanting to please others, to feed my need for approval. I asked God to heal the wound that lures me into overactivity. My self-esteem can be found only in God's profound love for me. Good actions and activities, if overdone, can be a way to flee God, to act as if we are in control of the world and, in other words, a temptation to be God. As I continue to pray to be healed, to unclench my fist and let go of my need for affirmation and approval, I am experiencing a new-found freedom. I am a work in progress, and old habits do not leave us easily.

We all desire happiness. God is not the enemy of our desires but seeks to satisfy our desires in healthy ways—to heal our disordered desires and meet the deepest needs of our heart. Good food and wine, physical pleasures, achievements, and affirmation, are all good things and blessings from God if we don't cling to them and make them our program for happiness.

Lent is a time to spend 40 days reflecting on where we are in our spiritual journeys, which of our desires are disordered and are keeping us from being free. What are some of our best intentions that trap us? What are the motivations behind our choices and actions? What self-centered demands and activities are driving us to fill the emptiness in our hearts? No amount of possessions, food, alcohol, or success can bring us happiness.

Where are you trapped and finding it hard to let go? That is the place God wants to work in your life and your compassion, growth, and ultimately healing.

Reflect

Jesus said, "One does not live by bread alone." What are you hungry for?

_____

_____

_____

How do you connect your life with the plight of the trapped monkey?

_____

_____

_____

_____

Select one of the three temptations—possessions, popularity, power—and translate it to everyday life.

_____

_____

_____

_____

Live Lent!

† Choose one of the temptations that most allure you. Reflect on the motivation and choices you make in light of that temptation. Ask God for insight and healing.

† Pray the Examen each night—the Examen is simply taking 10 minutes before you go to sleep to review your day asking God's forgiveness for any wrongdoings during the day and then thank God for the blessings of that day.

† Review your Lenten plan. What adjustments will you make in light of this reflection.

† Do an act of charity this week. For example, consider participating in CRS Rice Bowl, a program of Catholic Relief Services (www.crsricebowl.org). This project provides food for those who do not have access to it because of famine, natural disaster, or dire poverty. Look around locally to find ways that food is wasted—at supermarkets, restaurants, homes. Join with others to help remedy one of these situations.

 **Closing Prayer**

Pray together:

God of mercy and compassion,
forgive me for the times I fall into temptation,
release and free me from the trap of sin.

Give me the grace to be a more aware and self-reflective person,
a person who takes responsibility for my actions and emotions
and does not project those painful emotions on others.

Help me to let go of the false gods that I cling to and
give me a deep trust in your desire to fill the needs of my heart.

I ask this in the name of God who is a loving Father,
in Jesus, the compassion of God,
and through the Holy Spirit, the One who makes all things new.
Amen

Looking Ahead

To prepare for the Second Sunday of Lent, read:

- Luke 9:26-36
- Session Two: God-Moments Have the Power to Transform

Monday

Pray

"The ordinances of the Lord are true, all of them just." (Psalm 19:10)

Read *Matthew 25:31–46*

Summary: *"' Lord, when did we see you hungry or thirsty or a stranger or naked or ill or in prison, and not minister to your needs?'"* (Matthew 25:44)

Spend two minutes in silence. Then repeat this passage from Scripture, and let it speak to your heart.

Meditation

Many Italian men named Vincenzo who came to the United States during the great immigration of the late 19th and early 20th centuries were inexplicably called "Jimmy" in this country.

I knew several Jimmys as I grew up in a largely Italian-American neighborhood. In fact, there was one Jimmy whom I saw virtually every day—but it isn't a happy memory. That Jimmy lived in a shack behind a restaurant on our block, sweltering in the summertime and freezing in the winter.

For twenty-four years that I know of, and certainly much longer than that, Jimmy spent every day in that shack or within a hundred feet of it.

The folks who owned that restaurant kept him there as a source of labor: he pried open mussels—a specialty there—swept the yard, shooed the feral cats that haunted him, and barked at us kids if we got too close.

When I was young, he was a curiosity to me, but as I grew older and heard occasional disapproving remarks from my parents and grandparents, Jimmy's situation became more clear to me. He lived in a state of such loneliness that it became hard to look at him.

Jimmy's situation was no secret; people who lived in that neighborhood, including my family, knew about him; but he led a spare existence among the mussel shells and cats until he died.

At that time, in a small town, minding one's own business was considered prudent if not noble. It was a mindset that allowed us to neglect a man like Jimmy and congratulate ourselves for our discretion.

I suppose it never occurred to us to ask ourselves how this discretion, this resolution not to stir up trouble, squared with the Gospel we claimed to believe in.

If we had asked that question, we needn't have looked far for the answer:

"What you did not do for one of these least ones, you did not do for me."

Live Lent!

I will pay attention to my surroundings. I will take note of someone, acquaintance or stranger, who is obviously in material or spiritual need, and take the first step toward treating that person as I would treat the Lord.

 Pray

Lord, Jesus Christ, help me to see your face in the face of every person, to recognize in my brothers and sisters the humanity you shared with us, and to care for others as I would care for you. Amen.

Tuesday

 Pray

"Glorify the Lord with me, let us together extol his name." (Psalm 34:4)

Read *Matthew 6:7-15*

Summary: *"In praying, do not babble like the pagans. ...Your*

Father knows what you need before you ask him."
(Matthew 6:7-8)

Spend two minutes in silence. Then repeat this passage from Scripture, and let it speak to your heart.

Meditation

Albert Hay Malotte might be pleased to know that a song he wrote more than eighty years ago is still popular.

Malotte spent most of his career as a composer in Hollywood. He wrote more than 200 songs, many of them for movies, including the Walt Disney Academy Award-winning shorts "Ferdinand the Bull" and "The Ugly Duckling."

However, his most enduring work, composed in 1935, is a musical setting of the Lord's Prayer that has been recorded by dozens of artists ranging from Mahalia Jackson to the Beach Boys.

No musical treatment of the prayer has approached the popularity of Malotte's. Still, the composer has to acknowledge the contribution of the lyricist who, in this case, is the author of the Gospel of Matthew, one of the two evangelists who recorded Jesus' response to his disciples' request: "Lord, teach us to pray."

Malotte seems to have captured with his music the spirit of what is, by far, the best-known Christian prayer.

In this relatively brief prayer we proclaim that we are in awe of God ("hallowed be thy name"); we express our desire to live in right relationship with God in the here and now ("thy kingdom come"); we submit to God's will ("thy will be done"); we ask God to nourish our souls ("give us this day our daily bread"); we ask his forgiveness for our shortcomings ("forgive us our trespasses") and pledge to forgive others for any injuries ("as we forgive those who trespass against us"), and we ask for the strength to resist the lure of materialism and sin ("lead us not into temptation, but deliver us from evil").

The prayer is so familiar that we are at risk of reciting it more than praying it, and that suggests a worthwhile Lenten practice: reciting this prayer each day, pausing with each phrase to consider how it applies to our lives.

Live Lent!

I will say the Lord's Prayer each day in the manner suggested at the end of the reflection.

 Pray

Lord Jesus, help me to read and hear your words as always new, and help me to apply your teaching to my life here and now. Amen.

Wednesday

 Pray

"My sacrifice, O God, is a contrite spirit; a heart contrite and humbled, O God, you will not spurn." (Psalm 51:19)

 Read *Luke 11:29-32*

Summary: *"Because at the preaching of Jonah they repented, and there is something greater than Jonah here."* (Luke: 11:32)

Spend two minutes in silence. Then repeat this passage from Scripture, and let it speak to your heart.

 Meditation

A Benedictine monk in Missouri enrolled in a university art class and realized that with his clean-cut look he stood out among other students, who were, or were trying to appear, *avant garde*.

When a woman sitting next to him was asked by a friend who the monk was, she said, "Oh, he's nobody."

The monk smiled at this sign of a human tendency to care only about those who are like us and to dismiss everyone else.

That was the mentality of Jonah when God told him to go to Nineveh and tell the people there that they must repent or be destroyed.

Jonah set off, not toward Nineveh but in the opposite direction. As the story goes, the ship Jonah boarded was caught in a storm; agreeing that the storm was probably his fault, he let the crew throw him overboard; he was swallowed by a fish that had been sent by God and that, after three days, spit up Jonah on the shore of Nineveh.

Jonah reluctantly delivered God's message in Nineveh but assumed that these people wouldn't listen. He was disappointed when everyone, from the king down to the animals, repented.

In Luke's Gospel, Jesus spoke of Jonah as "a sign to the Ninevites." Jesus meant that just as Jonah emerged to preach God's word after three days in the belly of the fish, the Son of Man would emerge to display the glory of God after three days in the tomb.

Jonah is also a sign that God offers his mercy to all people and that he calls on us to be just as generous.

Lent is the ideal time to ask ourselves what individuals or class of people we regard as "nobodies" and pray for the wisdom to accept them as true sisters and brothers.

Live Lent!

As I read or listen to today's news, I will take note of men and women—or groups of people—whom I might be tempted to judge harshly. I will ask God for an open heart that, rather than judging others, embraces them as fellow human beings, made in God's image. I will ask God to extend his mercy to all of us. Amen.

 Pray

O God, you alone are the judge of the world. In your judgment, extend to me your mercy and give me the wisdom and generosity to extend mercy to those who offend me. Amen.

Thursday

 Pray

"When I called, you answered me; you built up strength within me." (Psalm 138:3)

Read *Matthew 7:7-12*

Summary: *"For everyone who asks, receives; and the one who seeks, finds; and to the one who knocks, the door will be opened." (Matthew 7:8)*

Spend two minutes in silence. Then repeat this passage from Scripture, and let it speak to your heart.

Meditation

Élisabeth Arrighi married Felix Léseur in France in 1889, but their bond was plagued by religious differences. Shortly before they married, Élisabeth learned that Félix had stopped practicing the Catholic faith. After their marriage, he became editor of a Paris newspaper that opposed organized religion, and the Catholic Church in particular, and promoted atheism. He also ridiculed his wife's Catholicism and for a while shook her commitment.

But eventually his aggressiveness caused her to delve more deeply into the faith, and she became profoundly spiritual. She wrote widely and performed such charitable works as her health would allow, but her primary focus became praying for the conversion of her husband.

Élisabeth died of cancer in 1914. After her death, Félix discovered her spiritual writing, which he had been unaware of, including a letter to him concerning her prayers for his conversion. Still skeptical, he visited the shrine at Lourdes and experienced that conversion. In 1923, he was ordained a Dominican priest; he served for 27 years. He devoted a lot of his time and energy to publishing and speaking about Élisabeth's spiritual writing.

Persistence in prayer sustained Élisabeth, and the example of her prayer evangelized Félix. Praying as Élisabeth did, and as Jesus urges us to, makes our personal encounter with God real and vital. When we express our faith in God by bringing our joys and sorrows to him—not demanding a certain response but submitting to his will—we find that he is not only the invisible Creator, but our most steadfast companion.

Live Lent!

My goal this Lent will be to focus on the person I am aware of who is most in need of prayer and try to pray for that person's needs for a few moments every day.

 Pray

O God, you know all of my needs before I bring them to you. Still, through prayer I express my faith that you are always present and attentive to me. Graciously hear me as I make my petitions, especially for those who have no one else to pray for them. Amen.

Friday

 Pray

"If you, O Lord, mark iniquities, Lord, who can stand? But with you is forgiveness, that you may be revered." (Psalm 130:3-4)

![book icon] **Read** *Matthew 5:20-26*

Summary: " 'But I say to you whoever is angry with his brother will be liable to judgment.' " (Matthew 5:22)

Spend two minutes in silence. Then repeat this passage from Scripture, and let it speak to your heart.

![candle icon] **Meditation**

When Tayseer Sarah died at 19 in an Israeli prison, his 10-year-old brother, Aziz, was among his survivors. Tayseer—jailed for throwing rocks at Israeli cars—had been a mentor to the youngster.

Aziz Abu Sarah took to throwing rocks, too, but later admitted that he did it mostly out of boredom.

In high school, Aziz worked for the youth arm of Fatah, a political faction in the Palestine Liberation Organization. He wrote and distributed pamphlets, risking six months imprisonment by Israeli authorities.

But after high school, Aziz decided to study Hebrew and enrolled in a class in Jerusalem. He was influenced by the teacher's broad view of the conflict and was inspired to examine all sides of the issues that roiled his homeland.

Aziz visited the Holocaust museum in Jerusalem, attended a Christian Bible college, and made friends with many Jews. He is now a partner in MEJDI Tours, which offers Christian and Muslim groups visiting Israel opportunities to meet Jews in contexts that reflect real life in the country. Aziz is also executive director of the Center for World Religions, Diplomacy, and Conflict Resolution at George Mason University in Fairfax, Virginia.

Anger over the death of Tayseer could have launched Aziz into a career of violent retribution that may have cost him his freedom and even his life.

Instead, in the spirit of the lesson Jesus taught in today's gospel passage, Aziz rejected vengeance and established at least a mutual understanding with Jews, who were his fellow Middle Easterners and his fellow human beings.

It's a good model to meditate on during Lent, the perfect season for letting go of whatever grudges we may be nursing. No matter how "legitimate" our grievance may be, the message from Jesus is clear: Let it go.

Live Lent!

I will carefully re-read the gospel passage. If it suggests that there is something I should do, I will do it before Lent is over.

 Pray

Lord Jesus, you urged us not to harbor anger against anyone. Help me to live in that spirit, forgiving in my heart anyone who has offended me, asking forgiveness for anyone I have offended, and, when possible, reaching out to reconcile from anyone from whom I am estranged. Amen.

Pray

"Blessed are they whose way is blameless, who walk in the law of the Lord." (Psalm 119:1)

 Read *Matthew 5:43-48*

Summary: *""For if you love those who love you, what recompense will you have?"* (Matthew 5:46)

Spend two minutes in silence. Then repeat this passage from Scripture, and let it speak to your heart.

 **Meditation**

The admirable moments in the life of Hubert H. Humphrey occurred almost to the hour of his death. Humphrey, a Minnesota Democrat, served as mayor of Minneapolis, U.S. senator, and vice president of the United States in Lyndon Johnson's administration.

When Humphrey, who ran against Richard Nixon in the 1968 presidential election, campaigned on "the politics of joy," he was ridiculed as though he were unaware of the racial turmoil besetting the nation. But that was Humphrey—the eternal optimist.

Humphrey was diagnosed with cancer in 1977. Knowing that he would die, he telephoned Nixon, who had resigned in disgrace from the presidency. Humphrey invited Nixon to attend the funeral and arranged for him to be placed among the highest-ranking dignitaries at the ceremony.

This gracious gesture did not mean that Humphrey had forgotten the acrimony that had colored his relationship with Nixon nor the behavior that had led to Nixon's downfall; it meant that Humphrey did not want bitterness to outlive him.

Nixon, no doubt aware that many would not welcome his return to the Capitol, accepted the invitation.

This episode is an example of the idea that Jesus expresses in the lesson recorded in today's gospel reading: "Love your enemies and pray for those who persecute you."

For many, this lesson is what the ancients called "a hard saying." It seems to contradict itself; how can one speak of "love" and "enemies" in the same breath?

The love Jesus speaks of here is not the love of romance or sentiment; it is the love of "letting go," the love of unilaterally putting aside whatever has fouled our relationship with another human being, the love modeled by a man who would say of those who were putting him to death, "Father, forgive them, they know not what they do."

Live Lent!

I will write on slips of paper any grudges I may be nursing or any hurts I still recall. If I am resolved to put these painful things behind me for good, I will tear up the slips and put them in my recycling bin, and then ask God to bless anyone with whom I have had differences in the past.

 Pray

Lord Jesus, when you tell us to love our enemies you give us one of the hardest lessons of all. Help me to discard any bitterness I may feel toward others and hear my prayer that they may find peace in you. Amen.

Second Sunday of Lent

God Moments have the Power to Transform

Suggested Environment

A small table with a burning candle and a Bible opened to the gospel reading for this session. Consider decorating the table with violet, the liturgical color of the Lenten season.

Liturgical Readings for the Second Sunday of Lent

GENESIS 15:5-12,17-18
"The Lord God took Abram outside and said,
'Look up at the sky and count the stars, if you can.
Just so,' he added, 'shall your descendants be.'
Abram put his faith in the Lord,
who credited it to him as an act of righteousness."

PSALM 27:1,7-8,8-9,13-14
"I believe that I shall see the bounty of the Lord
in the land of the living.
Wait for the Lord with courage;
be stouthearted, and wait for the Lord."

PHILIPPIANS 3:17-4:1
"But our citizenship is in heaven,
and from it we also await a savior, the Lord Jesus Christ.
He will change our lowly body

to conform with his glorified body
by the power that enables him also
to bring all things into subjection to himself."

LUKE 9:28b-31
"Jesus took Peter, John, and James
and went up the mountain to pray.
While he was praying his face changed in appearance
and his clothing became dazzling white."

Focus

God reveals himself in our everyday lives—sometimes in special intense experiences and more often in quiet ways to strengthen our faith as we face life's challenges.

 Opening Song (To download, visit ocp.org/renew-music.)

"*Transfigure Us, O Lord*," Bob Hurd

 Opening Prayer

Divide the group in two, and pray alternately from Psalm 27, with everyone repeating the response:

R. (1a)   **The Lord is my light and my salvation.**

Side 1:   *The Lord is my light and my salvation;*
                 whom should I fear?

                 The Lord is my life's refuge;
                 of whom should I be afraid?

R.   **The Lord is my light and my salvation.**

Side 2:   *Hear, O Lord, the sound of my call;*
                 have pity on me, and answer me.
                 Of you my heart speaks; you my glance seeks.

R.   **The Lord is my light and my salvation.**

Side 1:   *Your presence, O Lord, I seek.*
                 Hide not your face from me;

do not in anger repel your servant.
You are my helper: cast me not off.

R.   **The Lord is my light and my salvation.**

Side 2:   *I believe that I shall see the bounty of the Lord*
in the land of the living.
Wait for the Lord with courage;
be stouthearted, and wait for the Lord.

R.   **The Lord is my light and my salvation.**

The Gospel of the Lord

"Jesus took Peter, John, and James and went up the mountain to pray. While he was praying his face changed in appearance and his clothing became dazzling white. And behold, two men were conversing with him, Moses and Elijah, who appeared in glory and spoke of his exodus that he was going to accomplish in Jerusalem" (Luke 9: 28-32).

Read *aloud Luke 9:28b-36*

Reflect

What word, phrase or image from the gospel reading touches your heart or connects to your experience?
Share with the group, or write your response here:

_____

_____

_____

_____

Old Testament Connections

The Transfiguration scene in Luke's Gospel describes the prophets Moses and Elijah speaking with Jesus (verses 30-31). Moses was the giver of the Law, and Elijah was considered the greatest of the prophets. The three men talk about Jesus' departure from Jerusalem, a reference to his return to the Father after his suffering, death, and resurrection. The two Old Testament giants representing the Law and the prophets point forward to the Messiah and his sufferings. They validate Jesus as the revelation of God: On Mount Sinai, the radiant face of Moses reflected God's glory (Exodus 34:29-35), but Jesus unveils God's own face.

The Transfiguration was a revelation of God that happened on a mountain, traditionally thought to be Mount Tabor. Luke writes that Jesus took the three apostles "up the mountain to pray." The Old Testament describes many such manifestations of God on a mountain.

On mountains, the people of Israel came to know God's majesty, his presence among them, and his divine will (Exodus 24: 9-13; Isaiah: 2:2-3). On mountains, God revealed himself to prophets, deepening their faith and their understanding of his goodness and mercy. On the "mountain of God" in "a tiny whispering sound," Elijah heard God's voice and received his commission for the people of Israel (1 Kings 19:8-13). Isaiah exclaimed, "How beautiful upon the mountains are the feet of him who brings glad tidings, Announcing peace, bearing good news, announcing salvation, and saying to Zion, 'Your God is King!'" (Isaiah 52.7). Thus, on mountains, the people of God came to know God's righteousness and glory, for Mount Zion was "His holy mountain, fairest of heights, the joy of all the earth" (Psalm 48:2-3).

Another natural sign that often accompanies these divine encounters is a cloud, as it does in the Book of Exodus and in Luke's account of the Transfiguration. Clouds revealed God's presence to the prophets and the Israelites (Numbers 12:5-8; Exodus 16:9-12). After the flood, God said to Noah, "When I bring clouds over the earth, and the bow appears in the clouds, I will recall the covenant I have made between me and you and all living beings, so that the waters shall never again become a flood to destroy all mortal beings" (Genesis 9: 14-15). In a cloud over Mount Sinai, God summoned Moses to the mountain in order to show the people of Israel his power and to establish his covenant with them (Exodus 24:15-18). When Solomon created the sacred, inner sanctuary of the ark, "the cloud filled the temple of the Lord ... the Lord's glory had filled the temple of the Lord" (1 Kings 8:10). In a similar way, the mystical vision of Ezekiel describes how "The temple was filled with the cloud, the whole court brilliant with the glory of the Lord" (Ezekiel 10:4). Thus, the splendor and glory of God revealed in the Old Testament often takes the form of a cloud, symbolizing the presence of the Divine and the source of God's revelation for the sake of humankind.

To a Jew of the first century, the story of the Transfiguration, with its mountain and dark cloud, and the mention of Moses and Elijah, would be clear indications that a powerful God moment was about to occur. These experiences are called *theophanies* or intense manifestations of God's presence at special times and places. In some *theophanies*, as in the Lord's appearance to Abraham at Mamre (Genesis 18) or the angel wrestling with Jacob (Genesis 32:22-32), the appearance is in the form of an angel with no surrounding glory. Other *theophanies*, such as the pillar of cloud and fire that led the Israelites out of captivity in Egypt and the manifestation of God witnessed by the Israelites at Mount Sinai were awe-inspiring experiences of the glory-radiating presence of God (Exodus 19:1-20:26).

Theophanies are decisive events in which the presence of God is revealed in visible form through natural phenomena such as fire, clouds, storms, lightning, and thunder and in the voice of God. *Theophanies* thus bring the Divine Presence into an intimate relation with humanity, imparting God's message of hope and salvation and his power and glory (Genesis 18:23; Isaiah 40:1-11).

We, too, have theophany-like experiences in which we encounter God in powerful ways—in nature, people, and events. For me, these are special God moments that happen in everyday life to bring me hope and to strengthen my faith. A God moment can be a felt experience of God while watching a sunset, a peace that washes over us in a difficult time, an answer we've searched for long and hard, an unexpected visitor, births, deaths—countless otherwise ordinary human experiences. A God moment can happen anytime and anywhere and often when we least expect a palpable visit from God.

Reflect

What experience in nature helps you be in touch with God, aware of his real presence in the world: a sunset, the ocean or a lake, a mountain, a walk through a park—something else?

Share with the group, or write your response here:

_____

_____

_____

_____

 ## Meditation

The Transfiguration was a powerful experience for the three apostles in which God revealed himself to strengthen their faith and to prepare them for the trials and sufferings they would endure. They were on a mountain, prophets from of old appeared, and they were enveloped in a cloud. They knew they were in the presence of something greater than themselves—God's glory. The Transfiguration clarified for the three apostles Jesus' identity as the divine Son of God, foreshadowed his suffering and exaltation in heaven, and continues the apostles' training in discipleship.

This New Testament event has all the elements of a theophany. I believe God continues to visit us today in theophany-like experiences. I like to call them God moments. These are everyday experiences that are hard to explain but are not just coincidences or emotional reactions but, rather, God sightings. I recently had one of those theophany-like experiences at the bedside of a dying friend.

My recent God moment was not on a mountain top but on the top floor of my friend's house. It was the morning after RENEW's annual Gala—our biggest fundraiser. It was a wonderful event, but I was bone tired. My friend and colleague, Sister Honora, and I were discussing how much we had missed Barb, our faithful trustee, at the Gala. We had just learned that Barb, who had been suffering heroically with ALS (Lou Gehrig's disease), was dying. Sister Honora said to me, "I think we should go now." I concurred, and off we drove from New Jersey to Pennsylvania.

As we climbed the stairs, led by Barb's faithful friend Karen, I wondered if Barb would recognize us. When we entered the room, she lifted her head ever so slightly and gave us one of her smiles. She could no longer speak, but her eyes, slightly clouded, were still full of life. As I knelt by her bed, she grasped my hand. When I told her that we had brought her Holy Communion, she glowed. Barb was a daily communicant. We shared the Word and Holy Communion with her and just sat quietly in her holy presence. When she seemed a little anxious, we prayed the rosary with her. She instantly was calmed. I felt God's palpable presence in that room—the nature of our God as one who accompanies us in our darkest time became clearer. I knew Barb's suffering would soon be over. Two days later, she died the way she had lived—in the presence of her faithful God.

Karen shared with us that the previous Sunday Barb had insisted on going to Mass— weak and aided by a portable oxygen tank. The priest who was presiding at the Mass spoke movingly about Barb's tremendous witness in attending Mass and about all she had done for the community and the parish. The congregation broke out in applause.

The following week, Barb's wake was held in her parish church, followed by her funeral Mass. The church was filled with parishioners, students and colleagues from Bucks County Community College where she had served for many years, and with her beloved friends and family. Barb not only gave her life away for the sake of others, she also gave her death away as a sign of her incredible faith. Barb's courageous fight with her disease and the peaceful way she gave up her spirit to God strengthened my faith and that of the myriads of others who knew her. The faith with which she accepted her disease and her death makes me less afraid to face my own suffering and death.

When we have experiences we can't explain and think that we have felt God's powerful presence—that's a God moment. Even if it is just for a second, we know that something beyond ourselves has deeply touched our lives. When these moments happen, it is important that we share them with one another. Sharing these simple moments of grace can offer others hope and reassurance.

The hope presented by these God moments is that we will be

transfigured—changed just a bit to live more fully as followers of Christ, knowing more deeply that Jesus' identity and ministry cannot be understood apart from the cross and resurrection. Peter wanted to build booths and stay on the mountaintop. However, we, like the apostles, can't stop the clock or bask in the radiance of these tangible God moments. These experiences must move us forward with confidence that God is leading us, and that what lies ahead is even greater than what we have already experienced.

Reflect

The disciples do not immediately understand their mountaintop experience. Peter wants to build booths and stay on the mountain. What was Jesus trying to teach them through this experience?

_____

_____

_____

Share an experience of a God moment—many times, we don't recognize God-Moments right away. Sometimes thinking back on a situation, we realize that what we experienced was a God experience.

_____

_____

_____

How has a God moment given you more clarity and helped you with the tasks and struggles of everyday life?

_____

_____

_____

Live Lent!

† Pay attention this week to simple God experiences and share them with another.

† At Mass this Sunday after receiving communion, be silent and

intentionally pray that God's presence in the Eucharist be more real for you.

† Visit a sick friend.

† Jesus doesn't call us to live on a mountain top, but to serve God and each other "on the ground." Catholic Relief Services, one of the largest charitable organizations in the world, works to raise those who are poor to greater independence. Research the work CRS is doing throughout the planet, (www.crs.org, www. confrontglobalpoverty.org). Decide how you can best support this work and help others to learn about it.

† Review your Lenten plan.

 ## Closing Prayer

Pray together:

Loving God, we put our trust in your abiding presence in our lives. Strengthen our faith in times of adversity and suffering. Give us a new awareness of God moments in our everyday lives, and help us gain from these experiences a deepened desire to follow your will and way. Give us the grace to share with others how you are working in our lives. We ask this in the name of Jesus, the risen Lord. Amen.

Looking Ahead

To prepare for the next session, read the following:

• The Third Sunday of Lent: The God of Second Chances
• Luke 13:1-9

Monday

 Pray

"Forgive and you will be forgiven." (Luke: 6:37)

 Read Luke 6:36-38

Summary: *"Stop judging and you will not be judged. Stop condemning and you will not be condemned. ..."* (Luke 6:37a)

Spend two minutes in silence. Then repeat this passage from Scripture, and let it speak to your heart.

Meditation

During his 84 years, Martin Luther King, Sr. felt the full force of tragedy and hatred. He witnessed three lynchings when he was a child in Georgia; he was subject to the humiliations of the Jim Crow era; he lost one son—to whom he had given his name—in an assassination and another son, only a year later, in a drowning; and he lost Alberta, his wife of nearly fifty years, when a young man shot her as she was playing the organ in a church.

If anyone ever had a reason to be vindictive, it was Dr. King, but his response to the murders of his son and wife in particular did not follow what might seem like the logical script.

"There are two men I am supposed to hate," he said. "One is a white man, the other is black, and both are serving time for having committed murder. I don't hate either one. There is no time for that, and no reason either. Nothing that a man does takes him lower than when he allows himself to fall so low as to hate anyone."

Our reaction to such a story may be to admire a person who is so merciful, to regard him or her as a hero, and to doubt that we would react in the same way.

The implication of today's gospel passage is that a response such as Dr. King's should not be extraordinary—that all Christians, not just heroes, are called to be merciful in our hearts even toward those whose offenses are as extreme as murder.

Jesus gave us no wriggle room in this regard, no license to excuse ourselves for our harsh judgments because we are not heroic.

Jesus said what he meant: Be merciful, even as God is merciful.

Live Lent!

I will research programs through which citizens help prisoners through such means as writing letters or cards or giving books or subscriptions to periodicals. I will decide what I can do.

 Pray

Almighty God, justice belongs to you and to the public authorities who are responsible for fighting crime and keeping the peace. Give me the patience and compassion to forsake judgment and cultivate forgiveness in my heart. Amen.

Tuesday

 Pray

"Come now, let us set things right, says the Lord: Though your sins be like scarlet, they may become white as snow. . . ." (Isaiah 1:18)

 Read *Matthew 23:1-12*

Summary: *"Whoever exalts himself will be humbled, but whoever humbles himself will be exalted." (Matthew 23:12)*

Spend two minutes in silence. Then repeat this passage from Scripture, and let it speak to your heart.

 **Meditation**

A challenging quality of Pope Francis is the humility he has demonstrated in many ways, including his visits to prison inmates. The pope carries with him the dignity of his office and the teaching authority of the successor to Peter. The Pharisees and scribes of Jesus' time had similar attributes in their religious community.

Jesus didn't question that. Indeed, we hear him in today's gospel passage advising his audience to pay attention to what those religious leaders taught: it had behind it the authority of Moses. Jesus didn't urge his disciples to ignore religious law, but to teach it and put it into practice without exhibiting an exaggerated idea of their own righteousness.

This is the example of Pope Francis. Despite holding one of the most exalted positions in the world, he never creates the impression that he is superior to those he meets—whether they are the leaders of other religions, heads of state, ordinary people, disabled people, or convicted criminals.

When he visited prison inmates in Philadelphia in 2015, for example, Francis didn't present himself as the holy one who came to remind them of how low they had sunk. Rather, he presented himself as one who understood their struggle and in some way even shared it.

"All of us have something we need to be cleansed of, or purified from," he told them. "May the knowledge of that fact inspire us to live in solidarity, to support one another and seek the best for others."

It would be worthwhile during Lent to think of individual people or classes of people whom we consider somehow less than ourselves—regardless of the reason—and pray for the wisdom to replace any feeling of superiority with a desire for solidarity with all of our brother and sisters.

Live Lent!

I will pay attention to people who are in service positions—gas station attendants, busboys, checkout clerks, custodians—and greet them in a way that communicates that I consider them to be my peers and that I appreciate their help.

Pray

Lord Jesus, you opened your heart to people of all descriptions—the righteous and the sinful, the rich and the poor, the powerful and the meek, the healthy and the sick. Give me the same generous spirit, so that I may live in solidarity with all people as sisters and brothers. Amen.

Wednesday

 Pray

"Into your hands I commend my spirit; you will redeem me, O LORD, O faithful God." (Psalm 31:6)

 Read *Matthew 20:17-28*

Summary:　　*"Just so, the Son of Man did not come to be served but to serve and to give his life as a ransom for many." (Matthew 20:28)*

Spend two minutes in silence. Then repeat this passage from Scripture, and let it speak to your heart.

 Meditation

When I was teaching in college, a department head told me that she regularly received telephone calls from parents complaining about the grades their offspring were receiving. She told the parents that their offspring were adults and were solely responsible for earning good grades.

In a way, those parents were in the tradition of Salome, the mother of the apostles James and John; Salome wanted her sons to reap the rewards without doing the work: "Command that these two sons of mine sit, one at your right hand and the other at your left, in your kingdom."

Her sons, the Scripture suggests, thought this was reasonable.

The audacity of this request is made more egregious by the sequence of events: Jesus had just finished telling his followers that he would be mocked and flogged and put to death.

Even thought they did not yet understand that Jesus was God incarnate, Salome, James, and John apparently understood that he was destined to live in the Divine Presence and that his path to that destiny led through suffering and death. And yet, the two apostles thought they could join him in heaven without carrying the cross of discipleship.

The path that Jesus traveled, the path that James and John eventually did travel, is our path.

Lent, with its fasts and its acts of mercy and compassion, reminds us of this: We cannot be disciples of Jesus just if following him only means hanging around with him.

We can be his disciples only if we are alert to the needs of the people around us, do what we can to help fill those needs, and witness to our Christian faith regardless of how well or how poorly the world responds.

Lent reminds us, to paraphrase Nelson Mandela, that there's no easy road to heaven.

Live Lent!

I will take an inventory of the ministries in my parish, in the Sunday bulletin or on the parish website. I will make a mental note of which of these ministries I have supported, which ones I could support if I chose to, and how I could attract others to carry on the discipleship we have inherited from the apostles.

 Pray

Lord Jesus, you called your disciples to imitate you by carrying our own crosses in life. May I answer your call by extending myself in the service of those who are in need, seeking neither thanks nor reward,

and strengthened by the knowledge that you await us in your heavenly kingdom. Amen.

 Pray

"I, the Lord, alone probe the mind and test the heart, To reward everyone according to his ways, according to the merit of his deeds." (Jeremiah 17:10)

 Read Luke 16:19-31

Summary: ("Then Abraham said, 'If they will not listen to Moses and the prophets, neither will they be persuaded if someone should rise from the dead.'" (Luke 16:31)

Spend two minutes in silence. Then repeat this passage from Scripture, and let it speak to your heart.

 Meditation

We usually associate Charles Dickens with Advent, not with Lent, but the central theme of his novella A Christmas Carol reflects the point Jesus made with the story of the rich man and Lazarus. In the parable, we hear the rich man futilely trying in death to intercede for the wellbeing of his living brothers after spending a lifetime thinking of no one but himself. In Dickens' story, we hear the ghost of Jacob Marley warning Ebenezer Scrooge of the fate that awaits selfish people:

I was crossing Eighth Avenue in Manhattan with a friend when a grimy fellow approached and asked for money. He took me by surprise, so I pulled a bill out of my pocket and gave it to him.

When we reached the curb, my friend said, "Look back there, sport." I looked in time to see a policeman leading the beggar away.

"Now," I thought, "I'll spend the rest of my life wondering if that guy got arrested because of me."

I have since recognized something that I didn't notice at the time: when I gave five dollars to a stranger, I didn't ask his name. I remember that every time I hear the parable of the beggar at the rich man's door.

Many of the parables attributed to Jesus involve individual people—a king, a servant, a shepherd, a housewife, a planter. But Jesus names only one of those people—Lazarus, the man starving near the door of a wealthy household.

Clearly, Jesus chose that name because of its literal meaning: God is my help. A fellow human being wouldn't relieve the beggar's misery, but God gave the poor man comfort in heaven.

Some commentators believe that Jesus also named the beggar to emphasize the dignity the man was entitled to as a child of God—a dignity that the rich man and the rest of the community should have recognized and respected.

I missed that when I handed that man a five; he was just one more panhandler, but one who was hard to ignore.

May we all help those who need our help, not out of guilt or even out of sympathy, but out of recognition that they and we are equally beloved by the Creator.

Live Lent!

I will find out where in my vicinity there is a charity that assists people who are on the margins of society—unmarried mothers, drug addicts, those with mental illness, and homeless men and women. I will decide how I can help at such a facility during the coming year.

 Pray

Lord Jesus, help me to see with eyes like yours, and help me to love with a heart like yours. May I allow the destitute, the forlorn, the broken people in society the dignity that belongs to all of God's children, and may I do all in my power to restore them to wholeness. Amen.

Pray

"Remember the marvels the Lord has done." (Psalm 105:5a)

 Read *Matthew 21:33-43, 45-46*

Summary: *"The stone that the builders rejected has become the cornerstone."* (Matthew 21:42)

Spend two minutes in silence. Then repeat this passage from Scripture, and let it speak to your heart.

Meditation

I read a commentary by a Lutheran minister who said that observing his young nieces and nephews had taught him about "toddler property laws."

The gist of these laws was that if I like it, if I have it now, if I had it a little while ago, if I can take it from you, then it's mine.

And, the minister said, similar rules seem to govern a lot of adults—much like the tenants in today's gospel passage. Those tenants thought they could disregard the fact that the farmer owned the produce the way a child disregards the true owner of a toy.

Jesus told this story, in the Temple in Jerusalem, to religious leaders who had questioned his authority to teach and heal and chase away the dishonest money-changers and merchants who plagued the temple precincts.

Jesus told those leaders a couple of stories, including this one, to make the point that his authority came from God, whereas they seemed to believe that they governed the Temple and the spiritual lives of the Jewish people on their own authority.

The lesson in the parable of the tenants also applies to our everyday lives. Those tenants could have thrived if they had lived up to their agreement with the landowner. However, they came to grief when they ignored their true relationship with him.

And so with us: we can thrive spiritually if our lives are governed by the understanding that God creates everything and everything belongs to God.

We are stewards, and our right relationship with God depends on our caring for each other and for the earth, not only because the Master will some day call us to account, but also because we want to return the love that he has shown by giving us everything, including life itself.

Live Lent!

I will decide on one way I can serve the common good by improving on the way I protect the environment—such things as recycling and conserving electricity, gasoline, and water.

 Pray

Creator God, everything we have, including life itself, is a gift you have freely given. Inspire me to show my gratitude for your generosity by dealing fairly with everyone I encounter, whether in business or in private life. Help me to give generously and to take no more than I need. Amen.

Saturday

 Pray

"Bless the Lord, O my soul, and forget not all his benefits." (Psalm 103:2)

Read *Luke 15:1-3, 11-32*

Summary: *"But now we must celebrate and rejoice, because your brother was dead and has come to life again; he was lost and has been found."* (Luke 15:32)

Spend two minutes in silence. Then repeat this passage from Scripture, and let it speak to your heart.

 **Meditation**

When Karsten Mathiasen's wife told him that she loved another man, Torben, the couple had to tell their young son and daughter that their mother was leaving. Writing on the website "The Forgiveness Project," Karsten says that at first he wanted to harm Torben, but the anger subsided.

When Thanksgiving approached, he faced the possibility of seeing his ex-wife and Torben at a family gathering. Perceiving his daughter's anxiety, Karsten asked Torben to meet him for coffee; the meeting was amicable.

Next, Torben accepted an invitation to a birthday party for Karsten's daughter. Over time, the men became friends.

Years later, Karsten's daughter told him that she had learned from her mother that he had had an affair when the girl was only a year old. "How could you betray me?" she asked her father.

After a period of silence, he asked if she could forgive him, and she said, "Yes." Karsten became both a giver and a recipient of forgiveness.

When Torben was dying, Karsten was at his bedside and, knowing that Torben had had a difficult relationship with his dad, read him a story about forgiveness between a father and son.

While the dissolution of a marriage is tragic, forgiveness can limit the damage.

Just so, in Jesus' parable, nothing could reverse the consequences of what the younger son did; the wealth his father had worked for was gone. Instead of brooding, the father preferred to begin life anew, giving his son a second chance.

Our faith tells us that that is what God wants in his relationship with us. No matter how we offend him, he wants to be reconciled with us and, like Karsten and the father—who ran to meet his son—God initiates the reconciliation.

God is always eager to let us begin again.

Live Lent!

I will receive the sacrament of reconciliation.

 Pray

Lord Jesus, you preached and practiced forgiveness and reconciliation. May I imitate you by always being eager to discard hard feelings and begin anew in relationships that have been broken by me or by others. Amen.

Third Sunday of Lent

The God of Second Chances

Suggested Environment

A small table with a burning candle and a Bible opened to the gospel reading for this session. Consider decorating the table with violet, the liturgical color of the Lenten season.

Liturgical Readings for the Third Sunday of Lent

EXODUS 3:1-8a,13-15
God called out to him from the bush, "Moses! Moses!"
He answered, "Here I am."
God said, "Come no nearer!
Remove the sandals from your feet,
for the place where you stand is holy ground."

PSALM 103:1-2,3-4,6-7,8,11
He pardons all your iniquities,
heals all your ills,
He redeems your life from destruction,
crowns you with kindness and compassion.

1 CORINTHIANS 10:1-6,10-12
Therefore, whoever thinks he is standing secure
should take care not to fall.

LUKE 13:1-9
"But I tell you, if you do not repent, you will all perish as they did."

Focus

Jesus, empowered by the fire and focus of the Holy Spirit, urgently calls his followers to move from complacent faith to active faith.

 Opening Song (To download, visit ocp.org/renew-music.)

"Change Our Hearts," Rory Cooney

Opening Prayer

Divide the group in two, and pray alternately from Psalm 103, with everyone repeating the response.

R. (8a)   **The Lord is kind and merciful.**

Side 1:   *Bless the Lord, O my soul;*
and all my being, bless his holy name.
Bless the Lord, O my soul,
and forget not all his benefits.

R.   **The Lord is kind and merciful.**

Side 2:   *He pardons all your iniquities,*
heals all your ills,
He redeems your life from destruction,
crowns you with kindness and compassion.

R.   **The Lord is kind and merciful.**

Side 1:   *The Lord secures justice*
and the rights of all the oppressed.
He has made known his ways to Moses,
and his deeds to the children of Israel.

R.   **The Lord is kind and merciful.**

Side 2:   *Merciful and gracious is the Lord,*
slow to anger and abounding in kindness.
For as the heavens are high above the earth,
so surpassing is his kindness toward those who fear him.

R.   **The Lord is kind and merciful.**

ⓣ The Gospel of the Lord

""For three years now I have come in search of fruit on this fig tree but have found none. So cut it down. Why should it exhaust the soil?" He said to him in reply, "Sir, leave it for this year also, and I shall cultivate the ground around it and fertilize it; it may bear fruit in the future.

If not you can cut it down." Luke 13:7-9

Read aloud Luke 13:1-9

Reflect

What word, phrase of image from the gospel reading touches your heart or connects to your experience? Share with your group, and/or write your response here:

_____

_____

_____

_____

Old Testament Connections

Throughout chapters 12 and 13 of Luke, including this Sunday's gospel parable of the fig tree, the voice of Jesus is very much like the voice of the Old Testament prophet. It warns, sometimes in the most strident tones, but in the end reveals a loving God who patiently waits for the conversion of his people.

The thought patterns are linked closest with the Old Testament theme "The Day of the Lord." In the earliest Old Testament tradition, this day was to be a time of rejoicing, because God would bring to his people a final victory over his enemies.

Later, the prophets modified this ancient teaching to inject accountability into its meaning. It would be a day of rejoicing all right, but only for those who had been faithful to God. For those unfaithful, it would be a day of judgment, a fearsome finale of accountability.

For "fools"—that is, those without wisdom—the prophet Amos says the Day of the Lord will be a day of darkness, not light. It will be unexpectedly terrible as in the case of a man who scrambles away from a lion only to find himself in the arms of a bear! (Am 5:18-19).

The disciples of the prophet Isaiah, following the tradition of their master, described a terrifying God who, on the Day of the Lord, would descend upon the Babylonians. It would be retribution time for those who had unjustly punished Israel. The hand of God comes down as a thunderous blow, striking fear into his enemies; their bodies go limp, their stomachs become hollow. It is a day of wrath and fury on which few remain living (Is 13:1-22).

The imagery of a terrifying God on the Day of Reckoning is presented by the prophet Zephaniah who applies it to Israel itself. The passage (Zep 1:14-18) is an almost perfect parallel with the thought patterns of Luke's passages, where the people of Jerusalem are being warned of a sudden, immediate doom.

But there is still time to repent. If they gather together and "seek the Lord…seek justice, seek humility; perhaps you may be sheltered on the day of the Lord's anger" (Zep 2:3).

Thus, the basic rhythms of the Old Testament are again captured by the gospel passages. Fidelity to the teachings of Jesus is called for, a variation on fidelity to God's teachings in the Old Testament. There is a final time when the Son of Man acknowledges those who have been faithful and identifies the unfaithful. The time to change is now, before it is too late. However, we see in the final parable of the fig tree an all-merciful God who is ever ready to give his people another chance. Lent is a time to seize the moment to change and move forward on our spiritual journey.

Adapted from a reflection by Martin Lang in John: I Am the Vine, *part of the* RENEW Scripture Series.

Reflect
What motivates you more to follow the teachings of Jesus—fear of punishment, hope, love, or mercy?

Share with the group, and/or write your response here.

_____

_____

_____

_____

Meditation

On September 11, 2001, hijackers flew planes into the Twin Towers of the World Trade Center in New York City, and the Pentagon in Arlington, Virginia. In a field in southern Pennsylvania, a third plane crashed after passengers retook control of the cockpit; the plane was presumed to be headed for a target in Washington, D.C. Being from New York, I knew many people who were personally affected by this tragedy. I remember that churches were over-flowing for the days and weeks following the attacks. I had many faith conversations with the most unexpected people during that time. The sudden nature of the attacks brought home the truth that we don't know the day or the hour when we will meet the Lord—as you know from the passage above, the Old Testament calls this "The Day of the Lord." This tragic event moved us to pause and take stock of our lives. It was a call out of complacency and an urgent reminder that all we have is now!

The thread of urgency is woven through today's gospel passage and the passages that precede it. Jesus, empowered by the fire and focus of the Holy Spirit, urgently calls his followers to move from complacent faith to active faith—a faith that bears fruit through charitable works and just acts.

The message of urgency is brought home by the reference to an atrocity somewhat like our experience of September 11, an event that apparently was well known to people in the time of Jesus: The Roman prefect Pontius Pilate had slaughtered a group of Galileans who were at prayer. Jesus also recounts the story of the collapse of the tower of Siloam in Jerusalem that killed eighteen people. Jesus explains that those who were killed in both tragedies were no more evil than anyone else, nor were their deaths punishment from God. But death descended upon them when they least expected it. Jesus affirms that such calamities are not God's doing, but they do remind us how fragile life is. Experiences of life ending without warning can shake us out of our complacency. That is Jesus' message in this gospel passage. The time to repent and change our lives is now.

Jesus' preaching ends on a positive note. He uses the parable of the fig tree to remind us that we have a God of second chances. Though the fig tree had not produced figs for three years, the gardener was patient and held out hope that it would bear fruit. The fig tree was given another chance.

Have you ever wished you had another chance to do or be or say something? Maybe you wish you had another chance at a job, on a test, in a relationship, or to live in a manner more consistent with the Gospel—a life of love, forgiveness, and mercy. With respect to this last wish, there is no one who hasn't been given a second chance by God! Our God is the God of the second chance and third chance and fourth and fifth, and many, many more. God gives us countless chances to turn back to him so that he can transform our lives.

In today's gospel reading we have been given prophetic-like warnings with images of unexpected and violent deaths to urge us to live in a more Christ-like manner. But we are reassured by the parable of the fig tree that when we falter and miss the mark we have an all-merciful God who is ever ready to give us another chance.

Lent is a clarion call to change our lives—to live each day in such a way that we will have no fear of giving, before God, an account of our lives.

Reflect

How did the 9/11 terror attacks prompt you, or someone you know, to reflect on life and faith?

_____

_____

_____

_____

_____

If you knew when your life would end, what would you want your last day to be like? To whom would you wish to be reconciled? To whom would you reach out to express your care and love?

_____

_____

_____

_____

Live Lent!

† Reach out to someone with whom you want to be reconciled.

† Send a note to someone and express your care and love.

† Spend time prayerfully reviewing your Lenten Plan making any adjustments that you think are needed.

Closing Prayer

Pray together:

Lord, thank you for your great mercy
  and the urgency of your call to live as your disciple.

Thank you because, even when I mess up,
  you give me another chance.

Help me to bring the good news of your love to others
  so that they, too, may turn back to your love.

Give me the courage to shake off my complacency and choose this Lent
  to live more fully in your love and grace.

I pray this knowing that you desire the fullness of life for all. Amen.

Looking Ahead

To prepare for the next session, read the following:

- Fourth Sunday of Lent: The Waiting Father
- Luke 15:1-3, 11-32

Monday

 Pray

"A thirst is in my soul for God, the living God. When shall I go and behold the face of God?" (Psalm 42:2)

 Read *Luke 4:24-30*

Summary: *"Jesus said to the people in the synagogue at Nazareth: "Amen, I say to you, no prophet is accepted in his own native place. ... "Again, there were many lepers in Israel during the time of Elisha the prophet; yet not one of them was cleansed, but only Naaman the Syrian.' When the people in the synagogue heard this, they were all filled with fury."* (Luke 4:24-25, 27-28)

Spend two minutes in silence. Then repeat this passage from Scripture, and let it speak to your heart.

 Meditation

Home towns can occupy one place in our nostalgia and another in reality. For example, Jesus' home town, Nazareth, was a place of contradictions, as we read in today's gospel passage.

At first, the locals are pleased to have Jesus back among them, and they can't find enough good things to say about him. Then the mood changes dangerously when they hear Jesus say that his mission is not only to the people of Israel but to everyone, including those from Syria and Lebanon.

This statement would have shocked the worshipers in the synagogue, because the Jewish community had an insular vision. Their attitude was partly a function of the fact that they were monotheistic people surrounded by pagan cultures, and partly a function of the historic suffering of the Jewish people at the hands of one pagan power after another, most recently the Romans.

Jesus was introducing a radical idea, that instead of shunning people of different religions and nationalities we are called to reach out to them.

The woman of Samaria and the centurion whose servant was healed were converted after Jesus treated them with equanimity while his landsmen would have avoided them as "unclean."

Modern communications have nullified the effects of physical boundaries among nations and made it possible for people of different cultures to know more about each other than was ever possible. At the same time, social media and other digital platforms have been used to aggravate differences among nations, religions, and races, making the unity Jesus prayed for seem as remote as ever.

It is our place, as his disciples, to counteract this trend whenever we can by welcoming the strangers in our midst so that in the generosity of our hearts they may find the generosity of Jesus himself.

Live Lent!

I will do everything I can to make people whose ethnic and religious backgrounds are different from my own welcome in my parish and my community. I will not accept in silence statements and actions that demean or marginalize people of diverse backgrounds

 Pray

Almighty God, thank you for creating on earth a world of infinite variety. Life is enriched by your symphony of varying climates, terrain, vegetation, and wildlife. And I celebrate especially the men and women of so many nations, languages, and traditions. I rejoice in both their diversity and in their unity as your children, made in your image and likeness. May I always be an instrument of that unity, treating everyone as I would be treated. Amen.

 **Pray**

"He guides the humble to justice, he teaches the humble his way."
(Psalm 25:9)

 Read *Matthew 18:21-35*

Summary: *"'I forgave you your entire debt because you begged me to. Should you not have had pity on your fellow servant, as I had pity on you?'"* (Matthew 18:32b-33)

Spend two minutes in silence. Then repeat this passage from Scripture, and let it speak to your heart.

Meditation

We don't hear much about Al Hibbler, probably because he recorded his last hit song in 1957. Hibbler, who was blind from birth, was a "bridge singer"; his style linked rhythm-and-blues with pop. Six of his solo recordings made the charts, the biggest hit being "Unchained Melody" in 1955.

That same year, Hibbler recorded "He," with music by Jack Richards and lyrics by Richard Mullan.

"He" is a vague religious song that never uses the word "God" but attributes all power to God. Only "He" can turn the tide, calm the sea, decide who will write a symphony, and so forth. The lyrics also allude in a sentimental way to a personal God: "He still finds the time / to hear a child's first prayer / Saints or sinners call / and always find Him there."

It is the refrain to this song that evokes the theme of today's gospel passage: "Though it makes Him sad / to see the way we live / He'll always say, 'I forgive.'"

This idea is central to the Gospels, that God is always willing— eager, really—to forgive anyone who comes to him in penance. And, as Jesus says in the gospel passage today, we are called to imitate God in this inexhaustible mercy.

Peter thought he was generous by suggesting that he should forgive an offense seven times, because in that number-conscious culture "seven" expressed completeness and seven times was more than would be expected.

Jesus' answer to Peter—"seventy times seven" in some translations and "seventy-seven times" in others—means that there is no end to the obligation to forgive.

Jesus meant what he said, and Lent is a good time to apply his teaching to ourselves by letting go of the grudges and hurt feelings that may be weighing us down.

Live Lent!

I will prayerfully read today's gospel passage again and consider honestly which one of the characters in this story most closely resembles me. I will conclude by saying the Lord's Prayer.

 Pray

Lord Jesus, you have taught us that our willingness to forgive others should never be exhausted. May I have the patience and openness of heart to live up to that challenge, inspired by your teaching and your example. Amen.

Wednesday

 Pray

"He sends forth his command to the earth; swiftly runs his word!" (Psalm 147:15)

 Read *Matthew 5:17-19*

Summary: *"'Do not think that I have come to abolish the law or the prophets. I have come not to abolish but to fulfill.'"* (Matthew 5:17)

Spend two minutes in silence. Then repeat this passage from Scripture, and let it speak to your heart.

 Meditation

The last time I was stopped by a policeman, I was in Lake Mary, Florida, where I had made an illegal right turn at a red light.

We talked about the fact that there was no sign at the right-hand curb, where I am accustomed to seeing one, and that the sign on top of the signal itself was rather small. We also talked about the fact that the officer was from Denville, N.J., and that he was once a member of the same fire department as my wife's nephews.

He didn't give me a summons.

One might argue that, strictly speaking, the officer should have given me a summons, since I had broken the law.

The fact that he did not give me a summons flowed from the difference between the letter of the law and the spirit of the law.

The spirit of that particular law is a desire to keep people safe; inasmuch as nothing had occurred as a result of my illegal turn, and the officer had stopped me and made his point, the spirit of the law was upheld, and the letter of the law need not be applied. This distinction is at the heart of the message in today's gospel reading.

Jesus, an observant Jew, says that he has not come to set aside the Law of Moses—the covenant God made with Israel. For those who follow Jesus, that law is perfected in him—in its spirit, not necessarily in the literal application of its many specific provisions, including circumcision, ritual purity, and dietary restrictions.

The spirit of the Law of Moses is that God unconditionally loves his people and that his people are to unconditionally love one another with the same level of faithfulness.

That, Jesus said, is the *whole* law.

Live Lent!

Many people today are casual about speed limits, stop signs, and traffic signals—all of which are designed to serve the common good. I will show my love for others by observing the laws that exist to protect them.

 Pray

Lord Jesus, you taught us to love one another as you have loved us. May my love for others direct everything I do so that I never act selfishly but always act for the common good. Amen.

Thursday

 Pray

"Listen to my voice; then I will be your God and you shall be my people. Walk in all the ways that I command you, so that you may prosper." (Jeremiah 7:23b)

 Read *Luke 11:14-23*

Summary: *"Whoever is not with me is against me, and whoever does not gather with me scatters." (Luke 11:23)*

Spend two minutes in silence. Then repeat this passage from Scripture, and let it speak to your heart.

Meditation

It seems that no matter how ludicrous an idea is, someone will believe it.

Take the idea that the world is flat—which Hellenist astronomers dismissed some three hundred years before the birth of Jesus and some observers had rejected perhaps three hundred years earlier. Contrary to lingering mythology, Europeans in the 15th century did not think a ship would fall off the earth if it sailed beyond the horizon.

And yet, there are folks in the 21st century who argue that the earth is flat; in fact, there is still a Flat Earth Society. Such folks are unmoved by the fact that satellite photography shows the earth as a sphere, or the fact that people have circled the globe, beginning with Ferdinand Magellan's crew in the 16th century.

Pope Francis said that to have a fruitful dialogue we must begin by assuming that we all arrive at our opinions honestly. The flat-earth theory doesn't meet that test; an honest examination of facts cannot support it, but there are ideas about which the facts are not conclusive and there is therefore room for conflicting opinions.

But the fact that we are respectful of others' views and engage people of other religions in serious dialogue—as the Catholic Church does—does not mean that we waver in our acceptance of the Gospel or of its application to our lives.

"Whoever is not with me is against me," Jesus says in today's gospel passage; it's an important point to ponder as we examine our lives during Lent. Following Jesus means loving God and submitting to his will and loving other people, without exception, as though their wellbeing is more important to us than our own.

Jesus calls for an up or down decision from all of us: Are we with him or against him?

Live Lent!

I will spend time reviewing important decisions I made and actions I took during the past year. Was I for or against Jesus in each case?

 Pray

Lord Jesus Christ, I believe that your Gospel of love is the way to salvation for all people. Help me to live always, in large matters and small, in keeping with your word and example, so that you may always count me among your friends. Amen.

Friday

 Pray

"There shall be no strange god among you nor shall you worship any alien god. I, the Lord, am your God. . . ." (Psalm 81:10-11a)

Read *Mark 12:28-34*

Summary: *"'And to love him with all your heart, with all your understanding, with all your strength, and to love your neighbor as yourself is worth more than all burnt offerings and sacrifices.'"* (Mark 12:33)

Spend two minutes in silence. Then repeat this passage from Scripture, and let it speak to your heart.

Meditation

The Nazis' anti-Semitic propaganda backfired when it came to Albert Friedlander.

Friedlander and his family lived in Germany as the Nazis were launching their campaign to eradicate Judaism in Europe. He told author Karen Armstrong that as a child he knew how the Nazis tried to dehumanize Jews, and that he composed a list of the positive aspects of his character that contradicted the slanders against his people.

Friedlander made a commitment to use his moral and intellectual gifts to benefit the world around him. He was eight years old. He and his family fled Germany to Cuba in 1939; the parents and three children were separated for a time, but they were reunited in Virginia.

Friedlander graduated from the University of Chicago when he was 18, entered rabbinic school, and was ordained in 1952. He was a rabbi, teacher, and chaplain in the United States and in England and was active in dialogue among Jews, Christians, and Muslims.

Friedlander was admired for his patience, kindness, and wisdom, and for his vision of a universal humanity. The rabbi believed that he became such a man because he had learned as a child that no matter what the Nazis had to say about it, he was a person of value.

He had learned to love himself—the very thing implied by the commandment Jesus cites in today's gospel passage.

Quoting the Book of Leviticus (19:18), Jesus says, "You shall love your neighbor as yourself"—*as* yourself, not *instead* of yourself.

To love ourselves doesn't mean to be self-important but rather to respect the image of God shining in our nature; to reject any suggestion that we are evil or worthless. It means to avoid degrading our nature by harming or neglecting other people or the earth itself.

Live Lent!

I will thank God for the graces he has given me to both inspire me and enable me to contribute to the wellbeing of others; I will commit myself to continue making his love present in the world

 Pray

Creator God, the psalmist says that you made us a little lower than the angels and crowned us with glory and honor. May I always use the gifts you have given me to bless the earth and all living things. Amen.

Saturday

 Pray

"Have mercy on me, O God, in your goodness; in the greatness of your compassion wipe out my offense." (Psalm 51:3)

 Read *Luke 18:9-14*

Summary: *"But the tax collector stood off at a distance and would not even raise his eyes to heaven but beat his breast and prayed, 'O God, be merciful to me a sinner.'" (Luke 18:13)*

Spend two minutes in silence. Then repeat this passage from Scripture, and let it speak to your heart.

 Meditation

The 1995 movie *Dead Man Walking* is based on the experiences of a Catholic nun who counseled death-row inmates and campaigned against capital punishment.

One aspect of this complicated subject that was portrayed in the film was the inability of the families of murder victims to understand why the nun, or anyone, would be solicitous of a killer. That reaction is understandable in terms of relatives reacting to such a loss or in terms of an overall philosophy that requires a life in payment for a life—"an eye for an eye," so to speak.

But the nun, Sister Helen Prejean, was operating under the radical world view proclaimed by Jesus, namely that our relationships should be based on mercy, not on blame and guilt.

Today's gospel passage bluntly makes the point that a person cannot be righteous if righteousness is based only on his or her compliance with the commandments.

From what we know of Pharisees, the one in this parable probably was telling the truth about himself in his monologue about a blameless life. But his dismissive references to "the rest of humanity" and "this tax collector" reveal an incomplete morality.

Pope Francis explained why in his apostolic exhortation *Rejoice and be Glad:*

"Even when someone's life appears completely wrecked, even when we see it devastated by vices or addictions, God is present there. If we let ourselves be guided by the Spirit rather than our own preconceptions, we can and must try to find the Lord in every human life."

Cultivating this attitude in ourselves requires prayer and, as Francis wrote, an openness to the guidance of the Holy Spirit.

Live Lent!

I will consider in prayer whether any negative judgements I have made about others are in keeping with the lesson in today's parable.

 Pray

God our Father, through your Son's parables and example he has taught us to extend passion and patience to those whose lives, like our own, are not perfect. May I always respond to your Spirit prompting me to be guided by that lesson, regardless of the sins I perceive in others. Be merciful to me as I am merciful to others. Amen.

Fourth Sunday of Lent

The Waiting Father

Suggested Environment

A small table with a burning candle and a Bible opened to the gospel reading for this session. Consider decorating the table with violet, the liturgical color of the Lenten season, or rose, the liturgical color of this Sunday—known as Laetare Sunday. This Sunday gets its name from the first words of the traditional entrance antiphon for the Mass of the day, "Laetare, Jerusalem" ("Rejoice, Jerusalem"). We rejoice in the midst of the solemn season of Lent, because we anticipate the Easter celebration of our salvation.

Liturgical Readings for the Fourth Sunday of Lent

2 CHRONICLES 36:14-16, 19-23
The Lord said to Joshua,
"Today I have removed the reproach of Egypt from you."

PSALM 34:2-3,4-5,6-7
"Taste and see the goodness of the Lord" (9a)

2 CORINTHIANS 5:17-21
Whoever is in Christ is a new creation:
the old things have passed away;
behold, new things have come.

LUKE 15:1-3,11-32
"Then let us celebrate with a feast,

because this son of mine was dead, and has come to life again;
he was lost, and has been found."

Focus

Jesus shows us the Christian way—the way of mercy and forgiveness.

 Opening Song (To download, visit ocp.org/renew-music.)
"*Come Home,*" Bob Dufford, SJ

 Opening Prayer

Divide the group in two, and pray together from Psalm 34 with everyone repeating the response:

R.   **Taste and see the goodness of the Lord.**

Side 1:   *I will bless the Lord at all times;*
            his praise shall be ever in my mouth.

R.   **Taste and see the goodness of the Lord.**

Side 2:   *Let my soul glory in the Lord;*
            the lowly will hear me and be glad.

R.   **Taste and see the goodness of the Lord.**

Side 1:   *Glorify the Lord with me,*
            let us together extol his name.

R.   **Taste and see the goodness of the Lord.**

Side 2:   *I sought the Lord, and he answered me,*
            And delivered me from all my fears.

R.   **Taste and see the goodness of the Lord.**

Side 1:   *Look to him that you may be radiant with joy,*
            and your faces may not blush with shame.

R.   **Taste and see the goodness of the Lord.**

Side 2:   *When the poor one cried out, the Lord heard,*
            and from all his distress he saved him.

R.   **Taste and see the goodness of the Lord.**

■ The Gospel of the Lord

"His father ordered his servants, 'Quickly bring the finest robe and put it on him; put a ring on his finger and sandals on his feet. Take the fattened calf and slaughter it. Then let us celebrate with a feast, because this son of mine was dead, and has come to life again; he was lost, and has been found.'" Luke 15:22-24

Read aloud Luke 15:1-3, 11-32

Reflect

What word, phrase of image from the gospel reading touches your heart or connects to your experience?

Share with your group, and/or write your response here:

_____

_____

_____

_____

Old Testament Connections

Deuteronomy 21:15-21 contains two regulations about inheritance and about sons. The first regulation (verses 15-17) concerns a man who is to give his inheritance to two sons. The older is the child of a less-loved wife; the younger is the child of the better-loved. The father must not favor the younger, the child of the better-loved mother, but must give a double share of his inheritance to the actual firstborn, for that is his sacred duty according to the Law.

The second regulation is about an unfaithful son. It is shocking for us to hear: "If someone has a stubborn and rebellious son who will not obey his father and mother, who does not heed them when they discipline him, then his father and his mother shall take hold of him and bring him out to the elders of his town at the gate of that place. They shall say to the elders of his town, "This son of ours is stubborn and rebellious. He will not obey us. He is a glutton and a drunkard." Then all the men of the town shall stone him to death. So you shall purge the evil from your midst; and all Israel will hear, and be afraid." (Dt 21:18-21).

The teaching of Jesus goes far beyond these regulations. It seems clear that the story told by Jesus reflects knowledge of this passage in the Law. In the story that Jesus tells, the younger son is the one who asks for his inheritance. He would represent the child of the favored wife from the example in Deuteronomy. At any rate, the father indulges this son but does not break the Law. He gives only as much as the son is entitled to—one third of the patrimony.

The younger son then goes off into "a far country," that is symbolic of the gentiles, who kept swine. He squanders his father's money on dissolute living, just as the bad son of Deuteronomy did. But here the parallel ends. The unfaithful son of the Gospel discovers his hunger and his need. He becomes aware of his sins against his father. The unfaithful son of Deuteronomy never leaves home but nonetheless squanders his father's money and refuses to reform.

The gospel story would have us zero in on the father, joyously taking the son back, bringing him to the table with the entire family in attendance. It is a loving restoration. So, the teaching of Jesus places emphasis not upon punishment, nor upon a shocking example of public execution. Instead it sets its own shocking example of forgiveness toward a son who has in no way merited forgiveness.

The teaching of Deuteronomy views the sinner through the lens of justice. The teaching of Jesus views the sinner through the lens of familial love. They reveal differing images of God: the Deuteronomy view was for then, but Jesus' view is for now. This story is intended for all those sons and daughters who live estranged from love. A good Father awaits them. He has already forgiven their sins, but they must become aware of their need for his love.

Adapted from a reflection by Martin A. Lang in Luke: My Spirit Rejoices, *part of the* RENEW Scripture Series.

Reflect

The teaching of Deuteronomy and the teaching of Jesus reveal two different images of God. How do you image God? Has your understanding of God evolved?

Share with the group, and/or write your response here.

_____

_____

_____

_____

 Meditation

This well-known parable in the Gospel according to Luke is often referred to as the "story of the prodigal son." Helmut Thielicke, a German theologian, helps us to understand the story anew by retitling it, "The Waiting Father." Thielicke says the parable is not so much about a rebellious child as it is about a loving father who waits eagerly for our return when we have turned away from him. The parable of "The Waiting Father" is the grand finale of three parables in this Gospel that illustrate a God of mercy who does not conform to common conceptions of how God should act toward sinners. The parables tell of a shepherd who abandons ninety-nine sheep to save the lost one, a woman who turns her house upside-down to recover a small coin, and then the father in this Sunday's gospel reading who patiently waits for and joyfully welcomes his son who has wasted his father's inheritance. With these stories, Jesus presents an image of an all-merciful God and teaches us what it means to follow the Christian way. We are challenged to share God's mercy with others—not once or twice but over and over again.

One of my early ministry experiences was at a parish in the South Bronx in New York. One Friday, I was bringing communion to the homebound. As I approached the grounds of one of the large "projects" (apartment buildings for the poor), I saw a young woman begging for money. As I approached her, I noticed her skinny body, poor complexion, and sunken eyes. She was obviously a drug addict. I started a conversation with her; her name was Joanne. She told me she was at the end of her rope. She was addicted to crack and had resorted to begging and prostitution to feed her habit. As we spoke further, she shared some of her story. She grew up in a Catholic middle-class family and was a college graduate. She dabbled in drugs, starting in high school, but then became addicted to cocaine and then crack. She had been in numerous rehabilitation centers and programs. She also told me her dad was a religious studies professor at a local Catholic college. I bought her a meal and asked if she would come back to the parish with me. I offered to call her dad. She said she was too ashamed. Her parents had accepted her back many times, and she had busted out of yet another rehabilitation facility after they had warned that if she left the program she could not come home again.

Joanne began visiting me at the parish office. I didn't know how much longer she would live. I fed her and gave her access to the bathroom to wash up. Finally, I convinced her to give me her father's name and phone number. She could not bear the thought that her father would reject her, even though she said she wouldn't blame him. I called her father with some apprehension and explained that I had met his daughter. He sighed with relief. He told me he was waiting for a call and was glad it was not from the police saying they had found her body. He shared with me the long saga of Joanne's addiction and the toll it had taken on his wife and family. He said, "Her siblings don't want anything to do with her. They can't take having their mother's heart broken again." He added with a tired voice, "But I can't give up on her." Before he hung up the phone, he told me he was on his way to pick up Joanne—once again. The "waiting father" embraced his "prodigal daughter" and took her home.

The word "prodigal" means "excessive" or "extravagant." When we're talking about the prodigal son, we are using the term in a negative sense. However, the word prodigal can mean excessive or extravagant in a more neutral or even positive sense. This is how it applies to the father in the parable and also to Joanne's father. They both seem to be recklessly extravagant in their love for their children.

Depending where you are in your life, you may identity with one or both of the sons—or you may identify with the waiting father. The younger son leaves home and is excessive in the way he spends what was given to him. He plunges himself into self-destructive activities that alienate his family. He is separated from his parents— "lost," the father says. At the same time, the older son who stayed home is excessive in his resentment and sense of entitlement. He feels taken for granted and pushed aside. The father is excessive in his mercy. Every caring parent can identify with this father; because that parent has, at one time or another waited anxiously for a child to come home.

Place yourself in the story, and imagine God waiting with arms outstretched, running to meet you, inviting and cajoling you to turn away from your sinful ways; or imagine him urging you to let go of your unforgiving heart, or nudging you to give a loved one another chance.

Jesus shows us the Christian way—the way of mercy and forgiveness. The God of Jesus Christ, our God, is a parent-like God who seeks out those who are alienated and unloved, those who feel unworthy and ashamed, and runs out to meet them, embraces them, and welcomes them to the banquet of the Lord. We are called to do no less.

Reflect

At this time in your life, with whom in the story do you most identify? Why?

_____

_____

_____

_____

What does being waited for and then welcomed feel like? Tell a story of someone who waited for you and welcomed you.

_____

_____

_____

_____

Do you find it more challenging to seek forgiveness or to extend forgiveness? Why?

_____

_____

_____

_____

Live Lent!

- † If you are struggling with one of your children, or another family member, or a friend, reach out to that person and let him or her know of your unconditional love.

- † Develop a relationship with programs that reach out to alienated youth and brings them home—for instance Covenant House— and begin financial and/or emotional support.

- † Research how the opiate crisis in our country is affecting your neighborhood. Gather a group to talk about a way you can make a difference.

- † Spend time prayerfully reviewing your Lenten Plan, making any adjustments that you think are needed.

✝ Closing Prayer

Pray together:

Merciful and Waiting Father,
*   we thank you for your extravagant and reckless love for us.*
You are patient with our wanderings,
*   understanding of our lapses of fidelity,*
*   and desirous of our return.*
Give us the graces we need
*   to reach out to those who are alienated*
*   from our families, our church and from you.*
Teach us to be as welcoming and accepting of others
*   as we are always welcomed by you.*
We pray this trusting in your love for us,

in the name of Jesus, the compassion of God
and through the power of the Holy Spirit. Amen.

Looking Ahead

To prepare for the next session, read the following:

- The Fifth Sunday of Lent: Drop the Stone of Judgment
- John 8:1-11

Monday

 Pray

"You changed my mourning into dancing; O Lord, my God, forever will I give you thanks." (Psalm 30:12,13b)

 Read John 4:43-54

Summary: *"The man believed what Jesus said to him and left. While the man was on his way back, his slaves met him and told him that his boy would live."* (John 4:50-51)

Spend two minutes in silence. Then repeat this passage from Scripture, and let it speak to your heart.

 Meditation

It is estimated that more than 40 million copies of the Bible are sold in the United States each year and that more than 88 percent of Americans have at least one Bible at home.

That means that a lot of people have ready access to, among other things, the teachings of Jesus. On the other hand, an American Bible Society study showed that only a third of Americans say that they read the Bible once a week.

In an era in which church attendance and religious practice in general continue to decline in the United States, these figures raise the question: "Who is listening to Jesus?"

In today's gospel reading, we learn about one man who listened—a "royal official," presumably a minion of Herod Antipas and, therefore, the Roman Empire.

When this man, desperate over his gravely ill son, approached Jesus for help, Jesus gave what seems like a testy answer; Jesus lumped the man in with curiosity seekers, interested in healing and other miracles only as wonders, as though Jesus were a carnival performer.

With this remark, and with his refusal to go to the man's home, Jesus was testing the father's faith.

And when the father heard Jesus say, "Go. Your son will live," he passed the test because, without any signs and wonders, "he took Jesus at his word." His faith was affirmed because, as he later learned, the fever left the boy at the hour that Jesus had spoken.

Pope Benedict XVI taught that the Christian life is at its heart an "encounter with a person," with Jesus. We encounter him in prayer. We encounter him in the sacraments. And we encounter him in his word.

Lent is an opportunity to continue or increase our encounter with him in the Gospels—to listen to his words, and to believe.

Live Lent!

I will pick one of the four Gospels and prayerfully read it through, imagining myself actually encountering Jesus as the evangelist describes him. After each passage, I will pause for a few moments to consider what word or phrase struck me most, and how it is related to my life here and now.

 Pray

Lord Jesus, we believe that you did not walk among us only to abandon us, but that you live on in us so that we might encounter you in your word and sacraments and in the men and women who cross our paths every day. Help me to recognize especially that I meet you most intimately in the persons of those whose needs I address, whose pain I ease, and whose loneliness I dispel. By doing it for them, I have done it for you. Amen.

Tuesday

 Pray

"God is our refuge and our strength, an ever-present help in distress. Therefore we fear not. . . ." (Psalm 46:1)

Read *John 5:1-16*

Summary: *"Therefore, the Jews began to persecute Jesus because he did this on a sabbath."* (John 5:16)

Spend two minutes in silence. Then repeat this passage from Scripture, and let it speak to your heart.

Meditation

Jonce had an accident in which my car hit the back of the car in front of me when the driver slowed down to make a left turn.

Even though we were driving very slowly on a wet pavement, I was following too closely, so my car skidded into hers. Neither car was visibly damaged. A policeman arrived and gave me a summons for careless driving on the premise that the accident would not have happened if I had maintained the proper distance—ergo, I was careless.

When I went to court two months later, the prosecutor convinced the judge to reduce the charge to a non-moving violation. I paid a fine, but there was no impact on my driving record.

I was guilty of careless driving, but common sense and—I suppose—mercy prevailed.

There's a similar issue at play in today's gospel passage.

Both Jesus and the man he healed may have violated the letter of the law that prohibited labor—strictly defined in those days—on the Sabbath. But those who criticized Jesus for healing the man, and the man for carrying his pallet, saw the law as being greater than either mercy or common sense.

As Jesus taught in words and deeds, such rigidity is not the way of God.

Pope Francis expressed this idea by saying that "in life, not everything is black over white or white over black. No! The shades of gray prevail in life." The pope was not talking about relativism but about discernment, about exercising wisdom and prudence—and especially mercy—when deciding how to deal with a concrete situation.

It's a good lesson to remember as spouses, parents, neighbors, employers, or co-workers with respect to our judgments about other people—especially when we're a bit too sure of our own righteousness.

Live Lent!

I will think seriously about how my own view of laws and regulations resonates with the spirit of today's gospel reading. I will ask myself if my view is the same when rules are applied to me as when they are applied to others.

 Pray

Almighty God, may your commandments and the laws established by our religious and civic leaders always help us to live at peace with you, with each other, and with the earth. May those with authority over us always act with justice and compassion, and may I act in the same way toward my brothers and sisters. Amen.

Wednesday

 Pray

"The Lord is near to all who call upon him, to all who call upon him in truth." (Psalm 145:18)

 Read *John 5:17-30*

Summary: *"'Amen, amen, I say to you, whoever hears my word and believes in the one who sent me has eternal life. …'"*
(John 5:24)

Spend two minutes in silence. Then repeat this passage from Scripture, and let it speak to your heart.

 **Meditation**

Trying to trace a statement to its source can be fruitless. Take, for example, this statement: "God created man in his own image and man, being a gentleman, returned the favor."

That has been attributed to Jean Jacques Rousseau, George Bernard Shaw, and Mark Twain. In the play *Inherit the Wind*, it is attributed to Bertram Cates, on trial for violating a state law that prohibited teaching public-school students Charles Darwin's conclusions about the evolution of the human species.

Whoever said it, and many similar statements, meant that human beings have concocted various concepts of God—none of them valid—based on their hopes and fears and influenced by their culture, education, and experience.

The same thing is true in many cases of how some human beings think of Jesus. Some dismiss him as a myth, and others profess to respect him as a great prophet or a wise teacher and an all-around good guy—but nothing more, certainly nothing more challenging.

But our faith tells us that Jesus was not only an historical figure, but he was the invisible and indefinable God made visible and knowable—during his own human lifetime and now.

In the remarks recorded in today's gospel reading, Jesus expresses this idea, saying that he and the Creator are indistinguishable: "Whoever does not honor the Son does not honor the Father who sent him" (John 5:23).

That is why we take the Gospel to heart, because the Gospel is the teaching of Jesus, and Jesus teaches with the authority of God.

And so our Lenten reflection on how our lives meet the challenges of the Gospel is not simply a self-help exercise but a sincere and thoughtful effort to live each day more and more in imitation of Jesus and more and more at peace with God.

Live Lent!

God blessed the earth by living among us in the person of Jesus. I will spend time today assessing how my life reflects, or could reflect, that divine life in my surroundings.

 Pray

Creator God, you gave a unique gift to the world by living among us in the person of Jesus and making your will for us clear in his teaching and his example. May I never stop striving to imitate him in my relations with others and with the earth. Amen.

Thursday

 Pray

"They forgot the God who had saved them, who had done great deeds in Egypt. . . ." (Psalm 106:21)

 Read *John 5:31-47*

Summary: "(These) works that I perform testify on my behalf that the Father has sent me." (John 5:36b)

Spend two minutes in silence. Then repeat this passage from Scripture, and let it speak to your heart.

 Meditation

In 2000, a ten-year-old Nigerian boy died in London, England, after being slashed on his left leg.

Two young brothers were convicted only after several years and three trials. The first trial failed, because the only professed eyewitness—a 14-year-old girl—was disrespectful of the court and obsessed with collecting a reward. The boys were eventually convicted of manslaughter based on new DNA evidence. So, one witness, the girl, was unreliable; the other, the DNA, was incontrovertible.

Jesus' contemporaries would have understood that aspect of this case, because credible witnesses were an essential element of Jewish law at the time.

This, no doubt, is why Jesus, as we read in today's gospel passage, cited the witnesses to his divine authority: the witness of John the Baptist; the witness of the miracles Jesus had performed; the witness of the Creator ("This is my beloved son . . .." (Mark 9:7b); and the witness of the Hebrew Scriptures—"Then the eyes of the blind shall be opened, and the ears of the deaf unstopped … and the tongue of the speechless sing for joy" (Isaiah 35:5-6).

And Jesus' point was that his critics were aware of these witnesses, but still would not listen to him. No doubt there were many reasons for that, including jealousy, a reluctance to change, and an unwillingness to accept the implications of Jesus' teachings about selflessness and compassion.

We needn't dwell on the failings of Jesus' contemporaries. His remarks weren't preserved in the Gospel for the benefit of those critics, but rather for ours.

Jesus' words should encourage us to not only listen to but *hear*, deep within our hearts and minds, the witnesses in history and in our own time who testify to the defining fact in the life of a Christian: Jesus Christ is Lord.

Live Lent!

I will spend time today contemplating the witnesses that support my faith in Jesus, God and man.

 Pray

Lord Jesus Christ, your Father's voice, the prophets, the testimony of John the Baptist, and your works in your own time and ours, all lead us to adore you as our Savior and God. May my faith in you never waver, but grow always stronger in my heart. Amen.

Pray

"The Lord redeems the lives of his servants; no one incurs guilt who takes refuge in him." (Psalm 34:23)

Read *John 7:1-2, 10, 25-30*

Summary: *"'Yet I did not come on my own, but the one who sent me, whom you do not know, is true.'"* (John 7:28)

Spend two minutes in silence. Then repeat this passage from Scripture, and let it speak to your heart.

Meditation

I went to buy a lawnmower part, and the man behind the counter said, "Hey! It's the fugitive—the guy on TV! You look just like him!"

He meant David Janssen, star of a 1960s series about a physician wrongly convicted and sentenced to death for murdering his wife. He escaped and scoured the country searching for the killer—trying to keep a low profile.

I don't look like David Janssen, but I let the man enjoy the moment.

That fugitive, whose life was at risk, comes to mind in the context of today's gospel reading.

Jesus, aware of the threat to his life from a hostile establishment, went to Jerusalem quietly, trying not to attract attention, to join his companions in celebrating the Feast of Booths. This feast—Sukkot—was an occasion to give thanks for that season's harvest but, more importantly, to commemorate the years the Hebrew people spent in the desert, living in tents or booths as they made the passage from slavery in Egypt to freedom in Canaan.

But Jesus was soon taking the risk of declaring openly that he taught with the authority of God. Listeners who knew of the official antagonism against Jesus were startled. This risk-taking was heroic on

Jesus' part, but it was also an example for us.

In the secular and skeptical milieu in which we live, we risk indifference, ridicule, even open rejection if we say aloud that we are disciples of Jesus.

And yet, we are not called to skulk around in the shadows, professing our faith only when we are at Mass or among folks of like mind.

No, we are called, not to proselytize, but give witness, to let the world know that we live lives of charity and mercy and justice precisely because we are followers of Jesus Christ.

Live Lent!

Pope Francis says that the Church will grow, not by proselytizing, but by making itself attractive. I will think about how my life at home, at school, at work, or in my community can draw people to the Church.

 Pray

Lord Jesus, you said that your disciples would be known by "their fruits," by the way they serve you and their fellow human beings. May my works of generosity and justice identify me as your follower and attract others to become part of your body, the Church. Amen.

Saturday

 Pray

"Let the malice of the wicked come to an end, but sustain the just, O searcher of heart and soul, O just God." (Psalm 7:9)

 Read *John 7:40-53*

Summary: *"So the guards went to the chief priests and Pharisees, who asked them, 'Why did you not bring him?' The guards answered, 'Never before has anyone spoken like this man'" (John 7:45-46).*

Spend two minutes in silence. Then repeat this passage from the Scripture, and let it speak to your heart.

 Meditation

As I was settling into a new position early in my newspaper career, I discovered that the straightforward task of physically getting the daily comics into print involved a chain of seven people, although only three were necessary. I learned that the procedure had evolved over a long time, becoming more and more complicated, and that no one had ever questioned it.

But when I suggested that we cut four people out of the process, some of them felt threatened both because they were losing their places in an essential function and because, after all, the overpopulated system succeeded in getting Dagwood and Charlie Brown into the paper. In other words, leave well enough alone.

We see some of that mentality, though in a more serious context, in the scene described in today's gospel reading. The critics invest their psychic energy in defending the status quo—and their own positions—and arguing about whether Jesus' place of birth qualified him to call people to greater perfection in their religious faith.   The only voice of reason we hear comes from the temple police sent to arrest Jesus: "Never has anyone spoken like this!"

That was the point: what Jesus was teaching.

If his critics had listened with open minds, they might have understood that his focus wasn't on urging people to reject their religious heritage or give up their religious practices but rather on inspiring them to take their faith even further by living free of prejudice and exclusion and full of selflessness and acceptance—to become closer to God by imitating God.

Lent invites us to examine our own lives in these same terms—to ask if we are too judgmental, too rigid, too self-righteous, and too preoccupied with rules and structures to live the kind of expansive lives Jesus calls us to.

Live Lent!

I will consider whether some aspect of my life is just "good enough" in terms of the challenging lessons of Jesus. If so, I will do something, even something small, to make it even better.

 Pray

Lord Jesus, may I never be satisfied that I am doing enough to respond to your challenge to love without conditions. Give me the courage to grow ever closer to you by imitating more closely your life of charity and healing. Amen.

Fifth Sunday of Lent

Drop the Stone of Judgment

Suggested Environment

A small table with a burning candle and a Bible opened to the gospel reading for this session. Consider decorating the table with violet, the liturgical color of the Lenten season.

Liturgical Readings for the Fifth Sunday of Lent

ISAIAH 43:16-21
Remember not the events of the past, the things of long ago consider not; see, I am doing something new!

PSALM 126:1-2,2-3,4-5,6
The Lord has done great things for us; we are filled with joy.

PHILIPPIANS 3:8-14
Brothers and sisters: I consider everything as a loss because of the supreme good of knowing Christ Jesus my Lord.

JOHN 8:1-11
But when they continued asking him, he straightened up and said to them, "Let the one among you who is without sin be the first to throw a stone at her." Again he bent down and wrote on the ground. And in response, they went away one by one, beginning with the elders.

Focus

Jesus is full of mercy and compassion, and his followers are called to share his mercy with others.

 Opening Song (To download, visit ocp.org/renew-music.)

"Loving and Forgiving," Scott Soper

 Opening Prayer

Divide the group in two, and pray alternately from Psalm 126, with everyone repeating the response.

R.	***The Lord has done great things for us;*** ***we are filled with joy.***
Side 1:	*When the Lord brought back the captives of Zion,* *we were like men dreaming.* *Then our mouth was filled with laughter,* *and our tongue with rejoicing*
R.	***The Lord has done great things for us;*** ***we are filled with joy.***
Side 2:	*Then they said among the nations,* *"The Lord has done great things for them."* *The Lord has done great things for us;* *we are glad indeed.*
R.	***The Lord has done great things for us;*** ***we are filled with joy.***
Side 1:	*Restore our fortunes, O Lord,* *like the torrents in the southern desert.* *Those that sow in tears* *shall reap rejoicing.*
R.	***The Lord has done great things for us;*** ***we are filled with joy.***
Side 2:	*Although they go forth weeping,* *carrying the seed to be sown,*

they shall come back rejoicing,
  carrying their sheaves.

R.   **The Lord has done great things for us;**
  we are filled with joy.

The Gospel of the Lord

"Jesus went to the Mount of Olives. But early in the morning he arrived again in the temple area, and all the people started coming to him, and he sat down and taught them. Then the scribes and the Pharisees brought a woman who had been caught in adultery and made her stand in the middle. They said to him, 'Teacher, this woman was caught in the very act of committing adultery. Now in the law, Moses commanded us to stone such women. So what do you say?'"

Read *aloud John 8:1-11*

Reflect

What word, phrase of image from the gospel reading touches your heart or connects to your experience?
 Share with your group, and/or write your response here:

_____

_____

_____

_____

Old Testament Connections

The woman described in today's gospel reading was apprehended for the sexual act of adultery. According to Deuteronomy 19:15, at least two witnesses of the adulterous action, exclusive of the husband, were required in order to condemn the woman. This was to keep the husband from dishonestly accusing his wife in order to be rid of her. We can assume that in the case the Gospel describes, two witnesses had come forward and were part of the posse who brought her before

Jesus. Nothing is mentioned of her lover; perhaps he escaped, or perhaps the accusers wanted to place the blame solely on her.

In Leviticus 20:10, the death penalty is prescribed for adulterous behavior but leaves the matter of execution unspecified. However, in Deuteronomy 22:21 it states that stoning is the punishment for unchastity on the part of a woman who is betrothed (engaged, in our language). This passage from Deuteronomy has led some scholars to think that the woman in John's story was not married. However, Ezekiel 16:38-40 implies that stoning to death was a normal penalty for all acts of adultery.

There is some evidence that in the time of Jesus the Romans prohibited the Sanhedrin's (the Jewish religious court) from trying and executing offenders. This placed Jesus in a predicament—if he followed Jewish law and said the woman should be executed, he would have defied the civil authorities. On the other hand, if Jesus spoke against stoning her, he would have violated Jewish law. The religious authorities tried to implicate Jesus in their merciless judgment, "just" sentencing and death by stoning. But Jesus just stooped down and silently wrote on the ground and then, when pressed to clarify his position, said, "Let the one among you who is without sin be the first to throw a stone at her."

Jesus, teacher *par excellence*, did not give a quick answer. He quietly challenged the religious authorities, the crowd, and the woman to reflect on their own actions. He led them into a process of discernment. They made a new choice; the crowd dropped their stones, and Jesus urged the woman to sin no more. All walked away with an opportunity for forgiveness and healing. Jesus fulfilled the words of the prophet Isaiah: *"Remember not the events of the past, the things of long ago consider not; see, I am doing something new!"* (Is 43:18-19).

Jesus' treated the suffering and frightened woman with compassion. He invited the law enforcers to let go of their arrogant judgements. Most importantly, Jesus revealed the God of Israel who is merciful and gracious, slow to anger, and abounding in kindness (Psalm 103:8) even in the face of infidelity, including yours and mine.

Source: The Gospel According to John (The Anchor Bible, Volume 29, pps. 332-8) Introduction, Translation, and Notes by Raymond E. Brown, S.S., Doubleday & Company, 1970.

Reflect

How does Jesus reveal the God of Israel, a God who is merciful and slow to anger?

Share with the group, or write your response here:

_____

_____

_____

_____

 Meditation

This story of the woman taken in adultery is a clear expression of the mercy and compassion of Jesus. As the story unfolds, we are struck by the delicate balance between the justice of Jesus in not condoning the sin, and his mercy in forgiving the woman. He resists the zealots of the law and looks past the sin of the woman and into her heart. He doesn't ask her for an account of her actions, nor does he expect her to publicly declare her sinfulness. He refuses to impart the punishment the righteous crowd has called for—the death penalty. He simply says: "Has no one condemned you? Neither do I condemn you." The leering crowd is waiting to take part in publicly punishing this woman. These indignant zealots are interested in the letter of the Law and not in the purpose of the Law. They cling feverishly to the stones in their tightly clenched fists, ready to right a wrong through violence. The stones in their hands have hardened their hearts.

Most reflections on this story focus on the forgiveness of the woman and rightly so. However, there is another lesson in this story. Fr. Jim Conlan, a priest of the Archdiocese of New York and great preacher, focused, in his reflection on this story, on the religious authorities and zealots. He would ask, "Who is the first one healed in this story? No, not the woman, but the first one to drop his stone and walk away."

Many years ago, I brought a group of college students to work a couple of weeks at our (Dominican Sisters) mission in Jamaica, West Indies. We worked at a summer Bible camp for kids who came from an extremely poor and makeshift community called White

Wing. I conducted the Bible classes and assisted with any disciplinary problems. On the first day of camp, Samantha—a feisty six-year-old girl, barefooted with tangled hair and beautiful brown eyes—entered my life. Rock throwing, or "stone pelting," as it is called in Jamaica, was strictly prohibited. The first day, Samantha was brought to me, not because she had thrown a stone—yet—but because she refused to release the stone in her right hand. She kept it ready just in case she needed to protect herself. And, believe me, in her community she needed to defend herself. I finally persuaded her to release the stone, because it was the only way we would allow her to attend camp. I bribed her with a treat, and eventually she dropped the stone. We became fast friends.

Samantha was doing fine and enjoying all the activities and meals until day three when a couple of the boys teased her. She quickly picked up a stone and hauled it at one of their heads. She had a fast and furious throw and pretty good accuracy. The older boy jumped behind a big tree. The stone ricocheted off the tree and hit Samantha above her left eye. She began to bleed profusely and tore after the laughing boys. One of the male counselors picked her up, kicking and screaming, and brought her to me. We tried to tend her wound, but it was clear that she did not care about her bleeding injury. However, she did want to be released to throw the new stone she now held in her clenched hand. I finally just took her in my arms and held her tightly; she began to sob, and eventually she dropped the stone.

I cleaned her up and pled her case to the camp director. I got one more chance for Samantha, but she needed to stay with me for the rest of the week. So, Samantha became my Bible class assistant. While she was on the camp grounds, she never left my sight. One day, I asked the children in my class how Jesus would teach the kids in White Wing about the Beatitudes. To my surprise, Samantha raised her hand and said in *Patwah*, called Jamaican Creole by linguists, "No *stonin*, no *tievin*, no *lyin*" I encouraged the children to put that into a song, and they did. So, every class began with singing a new Bible ditty. I would shout out, "What do followers of Jesus do?" and they would sing in reply: "No *stonin*, no *tievin*, no *lyin!*"

Like the zealots in our Gospel story, Samantha let go of her stone—at least for the duration of camp.

Whether you identify with the guardians of public morality or with the adulterous woman, you need forgiveness and healing. At different times of my life and in different situations, I can identify with one or the other.

Jesus gazes into our hearts with compassion and quietly challenges us each day to "sin no more" and "let the one among you who is without sin be the first to cast a stone." It is time to drop the stone of judgement and condemnation and allow Jesus' mercy to envelop you. It is time to drop the stone of self-righteousness and arrogance and allow Jesus' compassion to fill you. The God who is slow to anger and abounding in kindness and compassion awaits you.

Reflect

Reflect on Jesus' treatment of the woman: was it a wavering about Jewish law and morality or ambiguity about sin, or was it a manifestation of a compassionate God? Explain.

_____

_____

_____

_____

Biblical scholars have different theories about what Jesus wrote on the ground—really nobody knows. What do you imagine Jesus wrote on the ground? What do you think caused the religious authorities to drop their stones and walk away?

_____

_____

_____

_____

Which character in the story do you most identify with? What stones are you still clinging to? What kind of healing do you need this Lent?

_____

_____

_____

_____

Live Lent!

✝ Is there someone in your life that you have judged and cut off from your life because of a moral failing? Drop the stone and reach out to that person.

✝ Spend time prayerfully reviewing your Lenten Plan, making any adjustments you think are needed.

 ## Closing Prayer

Pray together:

My Lord and my God,
    you who are slow to anger and
    abounding in kindness and compassion,
    pour forth your mercy upon me.

Help me to drop the stones of
    self-righteous judgment,
    and the stones of retribution.

Let me always look with compassion and empathy
    on the actions of others.

May I always leave judgment to you.

May I learn to choose forgiveness and love.

Thank you for quietly inviting me to drop the stones I cling to.

Give me the grace to be held in your abundant love
    so I may unclench my fists and be free. Amen.

Looking Ahead

To prepare for the next session, read the following:

• Luke 23:44-49

• Palm Sunday of the Lord's Passion: Jesus, a Suffering Messiah

Monday

 Pray

"Only goodness and kindness follow me all the days of my life; And I shall dwell in the house of the Lord for years to come." (Psalm 23:6)

 Read *John 8:12-20*

Summary: *"Jesus spoke to them again, saying, 'I am the light of the world. Whoever follows me will not walk in darkness, but will have the light of life.'" (John 8:12)*

Spend two minutes in silence. Then repeat this passage from Scripture, and let it speak to your heart.

Meditation

One of my favorite strips in the many *Peanuts* anthologies I have collected portrays a philosophical discussion between Charlie Brown and Lucy. Charlie Brown begins by asking if Lucy has ever considered what the world would be like if there were no sun. Yes, Lucy says, it's an intriguing question that can set the mind reeling: "This is the sort of proposition that can produce endless debate." And what, Charlie Brown asks, does Lucy herself think on this subject? And Lucy answers: "It would be dark!"

Indeed, it would, because the sun is the source of virtually all natural light in our world. But the sun, in spite of its magnitude and power, is not the real light of the world. That, by his own testimony, is Jesus, who came to show human beings the path that leads to life forever with God—a path of love, charity, mercy, and justice.

The Pharisees who heard Jesus describe himself this way were too intent on demeaning his teaching authority to understand that he was not aggrandizing himself but offering them and all people an intimate connection with a loving God. The Pharisees, as Jesus knew them, are gone from the scene, but many people in our own time still look everywhere except to Jesus for enlightenment.

As Pope Francis has reminded us, we who are baptized have a vocation to carry the light of Christ to those people, wherever we find them, confidently testifying to our faith and bringing it to life in our service to others.

Live Lent!

I will invite someone who has been away from the Church to attend one of the Easter Triduum liturgies with me next week. I will make my guest feel welcome in church and use the occasion to gently testify to the basis for my faith.

 Pray

Lord Jesus, you said that your followers would not walk in darkness. May I always walk only in the light of your Gospel and reflect that light for everyone I meet. Amen.

Tuesday

 Pray

"The nations shall revere your name, O Lord, and all the kings of the earth your glory. . . ." (Psalm 102:16)

 Read *John 8:21-30*

Summary: *"'But the one who sent me is true, and what I heard from him I tell the world.'" (John 8:26)*

Spend two minutes in silence. Then repeat this passage from Scripture, and let it speak to your heart.

 Meditation

Many years ago, my friend Dave saw this sign in the window of a barber shop: "If your haircut isn't being done by Nick, you have no one to blame but yourself."

Dave pulled over and went in for a trim. "After reading that sign," he told me, "I didn't think I had a choice."

That sign evokes an element in the conversation described in today's gospel reading.

The beginning of this chapter in John's Gospel tells us that Jesus was in the Temple teaching a large crowd. These people had sought him out in a holy place, and yet he spoke bluntly to them, telling them that they would die in their sins if they did not accept that he taught with the authority of God.

The implication was that he had repeatedly explained this to them, he had demonstrated it with penetrating lessons about divine law and with acts of compassion beyond the abilities of an ordinary human being, and that the truth should be apparent to them if they really understood their own religious heritage.

If you don't accept that I am the way to eternal life, he told them, you have no one to blame but yourselves. The evangelist tells us that although they had doubted him, he kept teaching, and they kept listening, and at last "many believed in him."

We don't hear Jesus in person as did those people, but he continuously and patiently speaks to us in the Gospels and in the teaching of the Church. It's up to us to listen, open to the influence of the Holy Spirit, and to affirm, or re-affirm, that we know Jesus to be both human and divine.

And knowing that he teaches with such authority, it is up to us to live according to his word.

Live Lent!

Each week, ideally on Sunday night or Monday, I will read the gospel passage for the next Sunday's Mass. During the week, I will consider how Jesus' teaching in the Gospel resonates with the events of my everyday life.

Pray

Lord Jesus Christ, may I always listen to your Gospel with the conviction that you teach with the authority of God, and may I always imitate the faithfulness and compassion you practiced in your life on earth. Amen.

Wednesday

 Pray

"Blessed are you, O Lord, the God of our fathers, praiseworthy and exalted above all forever; And blessed is your holy and glorious name, praiseworthy and exalted above all for all ages." (Daniel 3:52)

 Read *John 8:31-42*

Summary: *"'If you remain in my word, you will truly be my disciples, and you will know the truth, and the truth will set you free.'" (John 8:31-32)*

Spend two minutes in silence. Then repeat this passage from Scripture, and let it speak to your heart.

 Meditation

In the 1964 musical *Man of La Mancha*, Don Quixote makes this statement: "Facts are the enemy of truth."

The meaning of that line is still the topic of spirited discussion.

The statement may seem to contradict itself—that is, if "facts" and "truth" are always interchangeable. But one reading of Don Quixote's remark is precisely that the two terms are not necessarily interchangeable. In his case, he had overblown but admirable ideals of justice and chivalry, and his friends and family tried to tell him that he was a confused old man.

That was a fact, but the truth was that he *did* carry out those ideals in his dignified treatment of Aldonza and in his defense of her when she was being mistreated and, by so doing, set an example that should have embarrassed the self-serving people around him.

In today's gospel passage we find the same two terms at odds. The people quarreling with Jesus pelt him with facts: they had never been slaves, they were descendants of Abraham, and they worshiped God.

Those were facts, but Jesus pointed out the truth—that their status as free people (within the context of a Roman occupation), their genealogy, and their acknowledgement of the one God did not mean that they need not embrace his Gospel by renouncing selfish attitudes and behaviors and living as he lived, with compassion, generosity, and justice. Their idea of freedom was not answering to a taskmaster and pursuing their own interests; Jesus' idea of freedom was emancipation from the bondage of sin.

We all know the facts of our own lives. We also know the truth that Jesus preached with the authority of the Son of God. This season is an occasion to consider whether the facts add up to the truth that sets us free.

Live Lent!

I will take stock of the ways in which I subordinate the *fact* that I can do as I please to the truth that I, and we all, are called first to serve God and each other.

 Pray

Creator God, you distinguished us from all other living things by giving us a free will. May I always use my freedom to serve the common good, serving you by serving my neighbors and by caring for the earth and its resources. Amen.

Pray

"Look to the Lord in his strength; seek to serve him constantly." (Psalm 105:4)

 Read *John 8:51-59*

Summary: *"'Amen, amen, I say to you, whoever keeps my word will never see death.'"* (John 8:51)

Spend two minutes in silence. Then repeat this passage from Scripture, and let it speak to your heart.

Meditation

Whenever I administer baptism, I emphasize the first question asked of the parents in the liturgy: "What name do you give your child?"

I stress the importance that the ancients attached to names. I mention that authors of sacred Scripture make a point of defining names such as Eve and recording instances in which the names of figures including Abram, Jacob, Simon, and Saul were changed to confirm their roles in God's plan. And I recall that angels prescribed the names of Jesus and John the Baptist.

The Book of Exodus says that Moses, aware of the importance of names, asked God, "If I come to the Israelites and say to them, 'The God of your ancestors has sent me to you,' and they ask me, 'What is his name?' what shall I say to them?"

According to one translation, "God said to Moses, 'I AM WHO I AM. . . . Thus you shall say to the Israelites, I am has sent me to you.'"

Scholars connect this with Jesus' answer to those who asked him how he could have seen Abraham, who had lived perhaps 1600 years earlier:

"Before Abraham was, I am"—"I am" being an allusion to God's answer to Moses.

In other words, Jesus was identifying himself with God.

His adversaries took the answer to mean that Jesus was lording it over them.

But Jesus was telling them that God was not remote but was among them—not only as the invisible Creator on whom our existence depends, but also in the visible form of a human being, our Savior.

In our Lenten prayer, let us embrace that reality—that God came into human history in the person of Jesus who overcame death and still lives among us and calls us to be his disciples.

Live Lent!

I will cultivate the habit of silently talking to Jesus during the course of my day in order to heighten my awareness that, in the risen Christ, God is always at my side.

 Pray

O God who created us out of your boundless love, I embrace you not only as the source of my life but also as the Companion of my days, the Guide of my youth, the Friend of my journey, and the Comforter of my old age. May I always remember, in good times and bad, that you are near. Amen.

Friday

 Pray

"But the Lord is with me, like a mighty champion: my persecutors will stumble, they will not triumph." (Jeremiah 20:11a)

 Read *John 10:31-42*

Summary: *"If I do not perform my Father's works, do not believe me; but if I perform them, even if you do not believe me, believe the works, so that you may realize and*

---

understand that the Father is in me and I am in the Father.'" (John 10:37-38)

Spend two minutes in silence. Then repeat this passage from Scripture, and let it speak to your heart.

 ## Meditation

Since at least 1926, Mohandas K. Gandhi has been quoted widely as having said something like this:

"I like your Christ, but I do not like your Christianity."

I can find no primary source that connects Gandhi with this statement, so let's put him aside, take the remark at face value, and use it to reflect on today's gospel reading. This statement is a harsh judgment of Christians, implying that we do not practice the faith we profess. It's also overly broad, contradicted by acts of charity by individual Christians and by Christian organizations all over the world.

It's true, of course, that there is evil and neglect in the world despite Christianity, but the example Jesus gave with his own good works, the wonders he refers to in today's gospel reading, and with the good works he describes in the parables of the prodigal son and the good Samaritan, addresses us as individuals.

Jesus didn't cure every ailment and right every injustice; what he did do was act with compassion when he was confronted by human suffering. Moreover, he didn't only heal physical disease, he saw the world with compassion, regarding no one as beneath him by dint of class or creed or nationality.

Whoever made the caustic remark attributed to Gandhi was right to the extent that Christianity had not turned the world into a paradise, but he had no way of calculating what kind of world it would be without the actions, small and large, of the uncounted millions who have led unselfish lives because they have followed Christ.

During Lent, let us be grateful for the opportunities we have had and will have to enrich the life of one person at a time, an entire community, or the whole world, because we have faith in Jesus and try to live as he did.

Live Lent!

I will intentionally take every opportunity, no matter how small, to act as Jesus would.

 Pray

Lord Jesus, the world is still struggling to take up your easy burden and your light yoke of justice and love. May I be faithful to your teaching, letting it shape every part of my life, and may I spread your Gospel wherever I am. Amen.

Saturday

 Pray

"He who scattered Israel, now gathers them together, he guards them as a shepherd his flock." (Jeremiah 31:10)

 Read *John 11:45-56*

Summary: "But one of them, Caiaphas ... prophesied that Jesus was going to die for the nation, and not only for the nation, but also to gather into one all the dispersed children of God." (John 11:49, 51-52)

Spend two minutes in silence. Then repeat this passage from Scripture, and let it speak to your heart.

 Meditation

The conversation recorded in today's gospel reading occurred shortly after Jesus had raised his friend Lazarus from the dead, leaving the man's family, friends, and neighbors ecstatic.

But the joy was not universal. Some religious leaders worried that news of such events would attract more people to Jesus and provoke the Roman authorities to a violent response. Jesus' ministry had already irritated these leaders, and the high priest, Joseph Caiaphas, was perhaps his most determined opponent.

And so, Caiaphas told the people gathered with him: "It is better for you to have one man die instead of the people, so that the whole nation may not perish" (John 11:50).

We know what Caiaphas meant, but the author of this Gospel goes on with what may seem like a contradictory statement: "He did not say this on his own, but since he was high priest for that year, he prophesied that Jesus was going to die for the nation, and not only for the nation, but also to gather into one the dispersed children of God" (11:51-52).

The writer is implying that Caiaphas was not entirely in control of the part he was playing in this drama. The high priest was launching the plot that would lead to the crucifixion of Jesus. But the evangelist implies that, under the influence of the Holy Spirit, Caiaphas was also foretelling that the death of Jesus would lead to the transformation of the human family.

All these years later, that work is still not complete; the human family is fractured by petty jealousies between individuals, by prejudices based on ethnicity and religion, and by military and political conflicts affecting millions of people. We can prepare for Holy Week by contemplating what part, in our small circle, we can play and do play in making the human family whole.

Live Lent!

I will inquire about the relationship among the disparate religious groups in my community and consider what I might suggest that would increase understanding among them.

 Pray

Almighty Father, the human race you created has evolved into a mosaic of cultures, traditions, languages, and beliefs. But your Son longed for unity among people—that, different as we are, we might be one in love as you and he are one. May I always strive for that ideal, rejecting prejudice and reaching out to embrace all people as brothers and sisters. Amen.

Palm Sunday of the Lord's Passion

Jesus, a Suffering Messiah

Suggested Environment

A small table with a burning candle and a Bible opened to the gospel reading for this session. Consider decorating the table with violet, the liturgical color of the Lenten season.

Liturgical Readings for
Palm Sunday of the Passion of the Lord

ISAIAH 50:4-7
"The Lord God is my help,
therefore I am not disgraced;
I have set my face like flint,
knowing that I shall not be put to shame"

PSALM 22:8-9, 17-18, 19-20, 23-24
"I will proclaim your name to my brethren;
in the midst of the assembly I will praise you."

PHILIPPIANS 2:6-11
"Rather, he emptied himself,
taking the form of a slave,
coming in human likeness;
and found human in appearance,
he humbled himself,

becoming obedient to the point of death,
even death on a cross."

LUKE 22:14-23:56
"It was now about noon and darkness came over the whole land
until three in the afternoon....
Jesus cried out in a loud voice,
'Father, into your hands I commend my spirit";
and when he had said this he breathed his last."

Focus

Jesus, the suffering Messiah, offers his life for us and in turn calls us to offer our lives in love for others.

 Opening Song (To download, visit ocp.org/renew-music.)

"*Behold the Wood,*" Dan Schutte

Opening Prayer

Divide the group in two, and pray alternately from Psalm 22, with everyone repeating the response.

R.   ***My God, my God, why have you abandoned me?***

Side 1:   *All who see me scoff at me;*
           they mock me with parted lips, they wag their heads:
           "He relied on the LORD; let him deliver him,
           let him rescue him, if he loves him."

R.   ***My God, my God, why have you abandoned me?***

Side 2:   *Indeed, many dogs surround me,*
           a pack of evildoers closes in upon me;
           They have pierced my hands and my feet;
           I can count all my bones.

R.   ***My God, my God, why have you abandoned me?***

Side 1:   *They divide my garments among them,*
           and for my vesture they cast lots.

But you, O Lord, be not far from me;
O my help, hasten to aid me.

R.   **My God, my God, why have you abandoned me?**

Side 2:   *I will proclaim your name to my brethren;*
in the midst of the assembly I will praise you:
"You who fear the Lord, praise him;
all you descendants of Jacob give glory to him;
revere him, all you descendants of Israel!"

R.   **My God, my God, why have you abandoned me?**

The Gospel of the Lord

Then the veil of the temple was torn down the middle. Jesus cried out in a loud voice, "Father, into your hands I commend my spirit;" and when he had said this he breathed his last. (Luke 23:45b-46)

***Read** aloud Luke 23:44-49*

Reflect

What word, phrase or image from the gospel reading touches your heart or connects to your experience?

Share with your group, and/or write your response here:

_____

_____

_____

_____

Old Testament Connections

There are a number of Old Testament references in the Passion Narrative. Overall, they reflect a very specific purpose in the writing of this section of the Gospel: to show that everything that happened, particularly the horrible and tragic death of Jesus, was a fulfillment of what had already been written in Scripture.

Earlier in the Gospel, we were alerted to the theme of the forthcoming suffering when Jesus himself spoke, on three occasions, about the tragic future of the Son of Man (9:18-22; 9:43-48; 18:31-33). The triple prediction builds tension as Jesus undertakes his journey to Jerusalem. It also prepares the disciples for the challenges of following Jesus. In the first prediction, as Jesus starts out, and in the last prediction, when he has practically reached Jerusalem, the language is unmistakable: the Son of Man will suffer, die, and—on the third day—rise.

This theme is tied together after the resurrection when Jesus meets with his disciples and reminds them of the predictions, saying: "These are my words that I spoke to you, while I was still with you, that everything written about me in the Law of Moses and in the prophets and psalms must be fulfilled" (24:44).

The notion of fulfillment implies continuity with Judaism. The New Testament is conceived as the latest testimony of the Scriptures in which God has again revealed something tremendously important to humankind. It is significant that in the predictions of the passion Jesus refers to himself as the "Son of Man." But while that expression is used in several places in some translations of the Old Testament, the passage most associated with such New Testament usage is the Book of Daniel 7:13.

In Daniel, the Son of Man is often interpreted as Israel personified and in glorious vindication of its enemies. God's Son is therefore a heavenly figure whom people of all nations serve and whose power is everlasting. This imagery is in sharp contrast to the suffering Jesus in the Passion Narratives. However, it does correspond with the picture presented by Jesus when he is grilled by the Sanhedrin about his role as Messiah. Responding to their direct question, he replies, "But from this time on the Son of Man will be seated at the right hand of the power of God" (22:69).

Luke's presentation, therefore, testifies to Jesus being like Israel in its greatest moments, when it is suffering for its faith, as in the events described throughout the Book of Daniel. While this suffering is the height of injustice, Israel endures it with hope, and, in the end, the sufferers share the presence and glory of God. Two passages in the Old Testament are clear in their presentation of a suffering servant who is still able to hope in God. They are the Book of Isaiah Chapter 53:11b ("My servant the just one, shall justify the many, their iniquity he shall bear") and Psalm 22, verse 20 ("But you, O Lord, be not far from me; O my help, hasten to aid me"). We need to read both passages to capture the full riches of this reflection.

Each passage, with specific references being made for each, is incorporated into the Passion Narrative as a recurrent theme. When Jesus is betrayed by his own and when he is crucified between two criminals, he can be seen fulfilling the text of Isaiah 53:12: "Because he surrendered himself to death, and was counted among the transgressors, bore the sins of many and interceded for the transgressors." When his garments are divided we hear the echo of Psalm 22:19: "they divide my clothes among themselves; for my clothing they cast lots."

Jesus is clearly the suffering Messiah. That is how he represents himself to the disciples after the resurrection (24:26; 24:46). And that is how both Peter and Paul present him in the Acts of the Apostles (3:18; 17:3; 26:23). A suffering Messiah is a new idea for Israel. Its concepts of a Messiah were either a Davidic figure, a priestly personage, or a transcendent being. Visualizing Israel's Messiah as a sufferer captures, in a single image, the highest calling of God's people throughout the Old Testament: the willingness to suffer for the one they love, to suffer for the faith they love.

Enemies cause the suffering—not God. The suffering is, however, endured for God. That imagery is fixed in Christian consciousness by the cross. It is raised to an even higher level when Christians understand the teaching of Jesus from the cross as the call to forgive one's enemies, even those who take from us the most valued of all gifts, our lives.

Adapted from a reflection by Martin A. Lang in Luke: My Spirit Rejoices, *part of the* RENEW Scripture Series.

Reflect

Share an experience of someone who suffered for another or accompanied someone in his or her suffering. How does that person reflect Jesus, the suffering Messiah?

Share with the group, or write your response here.

_____

_____

_____

_____

Meditation

The story of Jesus' passion reveals a God who suffers with and for us. Jesus, the suffering Messiah, offers his life for us and, in turn, calls us to offer our lives in love for others. Jesus fulfills the highest calling of God's people by suffering in humility and in forgiveness for the people he loves and for the God he loves.

Since the time of Jesus, many have followed his way of the cross and have accepted the mantle of suffering for others. Most are everyday people who offered their lives daily for their families and communities, who stood up for truth in the face of injustice but have not been officially recognized as saints. A few have been canonized as an inspiration for us and a reminder that ordinary people, through the power of God's grace, are able to do acts of extraordinary love. All authentic love involves suffering.

Archbishop Oscar Romero was a spiritual leader who followed Jesus' example of combating the forces of evil through non-violence.

Every Sunday, Romero's homilies were broadcast by radio and heard across the country. Romero preached regularly that it was not God's will for people to be poor and to suffer injustice. He spoke against the violence that was being imposed on the people. The day before Romero died, he preached in the cathedral what many believed to be the equivalent of his own death sentence. He called on members of the Salvadoran army to disobey their superiors and "lay down their arms and listen to the voice of God." In the eyes of his enemies, Romero had gone too far.

The next evening, March 24, 1980, he celebrated the evening Mass in the Hospital de la Divina Providencia in memory of an assassinated journalist, with a congregation of 25 people. During the Mass, Romero providentially proclaimed the passage from Chapter 12 of the Gospel of John in which Jesus tells the metaphor of the grain of wheat that must die in order to bear fruit. Romero's last words, just minutes before his death, were, "Those who surrender to the service of the poor through love of Christ will live like the grain of wheat that dies. It only apparently dies. If it were not to die, it would remain a solitary grain. The harvest comes because of the grain that dies…." Romero spoke of the need to take risks for the kingdom of God; he shared his vision of a new human family and pointed out that to achieve this we must be willing to suffer for peace and justice.

During the consecration, a gunman pulled up at the chapel, got out of the car, and stepped inside. Romero saw him take aim and fire. Archbishop Romero died while doing what he did each day during Mass—offering himself with Christ so all creation might be reconciled with God, and all sins might be forgiven. Like the death of Jesus, the death of the archbishop was a moment in which the separation between heaven and earth became very thin. The heavens became dark and on earth the veil of the temple was rent. God was present in the bleeding and dying body of Oscar Romero.

Archbishop Romero was assassinated for standing in solidarity with the poor and suffering people of El Salvador. Like Jesus, he did not seek to solve the problem of violence by responding with more violence but rather by absorbing it in suffering love. Oscar Romero was murdered during Lent 1980 while celebrating Mass in a chapel at the hospital where he resided. On Palm Sunday, six days later, his funeral Mass was celebrated at Holy Savior Cathedral in El Salvador's capital city of San Salvador. Throngs of people gathered at the funeral for this shepherd who was known for bearing his people's burdens and sacrificing himself for them.

He was proclaimed a saint by Pope Francis on October 14, 2018. The cause for his canonization languished for many years because his commitment to the poor and his opposition to the government were construed by some churchmen as political. But the people of El Salvador, from the moment of his death, recognized and celebrated him as a martyr for the faith—a saint.

On a visit to El Salvador, I once visited the humble room where Archbishop Romero lived and the chapel in which he was killed. Romero chose to live in a room on the grounds of the Carmelite Sisters' cancer hospital, surrounded by the poor and sick, rather than the bishop's palace next to the cathedral. I was struck by the few things in his room: a cot, a desk with a Pieta and a typewriter still on it. It was hard to look at the bloody vestments from the day he was slain, preserved in a glass wardrobe.

A Carmelite sister had recorded the Mass at which he was murdered. During my visit, I listened to Romero's last words while I was praying in that chapel. It was a powerful moment—his passion and suffering were way too real. The cost of authentic discipleship shook me to the core as I heard the gunshots. Do I have the courage to take the gospel mandate seriously—"If anyone wishes to come after me, he must deny himself and take up his cross daily and follow me" (9:23)?

Oscar Romero followed Jesus—the one who suffered in order to teach us how to overcome the violent and dark impulses within us and within our society. Oscar Romero was martyred and declared a saint. His voice could not be silenced by a bullet; in fact, it, has been amplified. He is a symbol of hope for all who have suffered poverty, injustice, and violence. He is an inspiration for those of us who want the courage to follow Jesus more authentically. As followers of Jesus, we will not be defeated by the power of darkness. We will bring the light of Christ to our world.

Reflect

Share something you know about St. Oscar Romero. How are his life and death inspirations to you?

_____

_____

_____

_____

_____

How and why is St. Oscar Romero a martyr? In what sense can it be said that he died for his faith?

_____

_____

_____

_____

Name some of the violent and dark impulses within our society. How can we, as followers of Jesus, bring light and hope to any of these situations?

_____

_____

_____

_____

Live Lent!

† Read and reflect on a book about St. Oscar Romero. Suggested titles include Oscar Romero: Reflections on his Life and Writings (Orbis Books); Romero—A Life by James Brockman, SJ (Orbis Books); Oscar Romero—Prophet of Hope by Roberto Morozzo della Rocca (Pauline Books); and Oscar Romero and the Communion of Saints by Scott Wright (Orbis Books).

† Watch a movie about St. Oscar Romero—such as with Raul Julia. Consider showing the movie at your parish and having a follow-up discussion.

† Attend one or more of the Holy Week Services: Holy Thursday (Mass of the Lord's Supper), Good Friday, the Easter Vigil.

✝ Closing Prayer

Pray together:

Suffering God, open our hearts to the many abuses of human life, liberty, and dignity.

We believe that in each person is found the Creator's image and that everyone who tramples it offends God. As holy defender of God's rights and of his images, the Church is called to cry out. It endures as spittle in its face, as lashes on its back, as the cross in its passion, all that human beings suffer, even unbelievers. Whoever tortures a human being, whoever outrages a human being, abuses God's image. The Church takes as its own that cross, that martyrdom. Give us the courage to accompany those who suffer, speak truth, and fight injustice in the name of Jesus, the suffering Messiah. (Based on Saint Oscar Romero's words from December 31, 1977, in the compendium The Violence of Love)..

St. Oscar Romero, pray for us. Amen.

Monday

 Pray

"I, the Lord, have called you for the victory of justice, I have grasped you by the hand; I formed you, and set you as a covenant of the people, a light for the nations. . . ." (Isaiah 42:6)

 Read *John 12:1-11*

Summary: *"You always have the poor with you, but you do not always have me." (John 12:8)*

Spend two minutes in silence. Then repeat this passage from Scripture, and let it speak to your heart.

 Meditation

"I love a parade," lyricist Ted Koehler wrote in 1931, "the tramping of feet, I love every beat I hear of a drum."

We all love a parade, but maybe not every parade. The Jewish people who lived in Jerusalem at the time of Jesus probably didn't love the parade Pontius Pilate put on every year.

According to scripture scholars Marcus Borg and John Dominic Crossin, the Roman governor staged a triumphal procession into the city every year around Passover to remind residents and holiday visitors of two things: the empire was in charge, and the emperor was divine—a god.

The same writers cast Jesus' entry into the city, riding on a donkey, as a deliberate contrast to the brazen military display by the Romans.

The empire that was then personified in Tiberius Caesar is long gone, but the Church—that is, the community that assembled around Jesus—has endured both persecution by a succession of earthly powers and weaknesses of various kinds in its own ranks.

The Jewish people, too—who begin their celebration of Passover today—survived the Roman Empire and the other despotic forces, including the Nazis, that have sought to annihilate them. It's important to keep this in mind as we commemorate the violence inflicted on Jesus.

But the fact that the Church and the Jewish people have outlasted so many determined enemies is not a reason for complacency. Christians and Jews continue to be persecuted today.

Let us pray this week for an end to their suffering and for the enlightenment of those who attack them.

Live Lent!

I will speak out against, and I will not condone by my silence, prejudice or intolerance of any kind toward anyone.

 Pray

Almighty God, please protect people who worship you and seek to honor your will by creating a society of justice and love. Soften the hearts of those who persecute your faithful ones, and lead us all toward a more peaceful world. Amen.

Tuesday

 Pray

"My mouth shall declare your justice, day by day your salvation." (Psalm 71:15)

 Read *John 13:21-33, 36-38*

Summary: *"Simon Peter said to him, 'Master, where are you going?' Jesus answered him, 'Where I am going, you cannot follow me now, though you will follow later.'"* (John 13:36)

Spend two minutes in silence. Then repeat this passage from Scripture, and let it speak to your heart.

 **Meditation**

The novelist Suzanne Collins wrote in The Hunger Games that "in order for there to be betrayal, there would have to have been trust first."

That certainly applies to the two betrayers we read about in today's gospel passage: the apostles Judas and Peter. Both of them had spent three years, virtually every day, in the company of Jesus. In fact, Jesus had chosen both of them as members of his inner circle. And yet, at the critical moment, both betrayed his trust.

Of the two men, Judas has the more complicated story—first, because there are contradictory and incomplete interpretations of his motives and, second, because, as far as we know, he never repented. We are left to wonder how he could have missed so completely the identity of Jesus and the truth of his teaching, especially his teaching on repentance and mercy.

Peter, on the other hand, embraced both Jesus and his teaching, although Peter had trouble accepting the inevitability of suffering—in the world at large and in the life of the Messiah himself. And Peter's betrayal would not be an overt rejection of who Jesus was and what he taught but rather a desperate act of self-preservation.

As Jesus predicted, Peter would deny the Lord three times, but Peter would also believe and preach the resurrection and eventually devote himself to the Church and give his life for the Lord.

We ourselves betray Jesus whenever we don't live what we profess to believe as his disciples, whenever we do not treat each other and the earth with the selfless care and compassion he practiced and preached.

Let us pray during this holy week that our role model will be Peter, not Judas—that when we have failed we will always turn to Jesus for forgiveness and rely on his inexhaustible mercy.

Live Lent!

I will conclude my Lenten observance by reserving time to pray quietly, laying at the Lord's feet, once and for all, any guilt or remorse or regret

I may be harboring, and accepting his unconditional forgiveness and invitation to begin again. Amen.

 Pray

Lord Jesus Christ, we all may betray you in small ways and large. May I always remember that you will never reject my penitence but will absolve me of my failings and rejoice in my resolve to never offend you again. Amen.

Wednesday

 Pray

"I will praise the name of God in song, and I will glorify him with thanksgiving. … 'See, you lowly ones, and be glad; you who seek God, may your hearts revive!'" (Psalm 69:31, 33)

 Read *Matthew 26:14-25*

Summary: *"The Son of Man indeed goes, as it is written of him, but woe to that man by whom the Son of Man is betrayed. It would be better for that man if he had never been born.'" (Matthew 26:24)*

Spend two minutes in silence. Then repeat this passage from Scripture, and let it speak to your heart.

 Meditation

As I was about to begin writing this reflection, I realized that I might have been misreading a statement attributed to Jesus in today's gospel passage.

The statement, as it appears in the New Revised Standard Version of the Bible reads as follows: "The Son of Man goes as it is written of him, but woe to that one by whom the Son of Man is betrayed! It would have been better for that one not to have been born."

I have been reading that to refer to the severity of the punishment in store for Judas Iscariot. But this morning I read in a footnote in the *New American Bible* that this expression means that "the enormity of the deed is such that it would be better not to exist than to do it."

That makes sense, because one thing we know about Jesus is that mercy, not punishment, was his top priority. After all, the implication of the Gospels is that Jesus anticipated what Judas was going to do; and yet, we find Judas still among "the Twelve," not only celebrating Passover but also sharing in the first Eucharist.

Judas is a mysterious character; we are not certain what was going on in his mind. But we do know that he had the same free will as do all human beings. His presence among the apostles at this late hour suggests to me both patience and hope on the part of Jesus.

Let us pray as we approach the end of our Lenten observance that when we are not fully faithful to the Gospel, Jesus will regard us with optimism and unlimited patience.

Live Lent!

I will resolve to be the patient presence of Jesus to everyone I encounter, including those who may disagree with me or disrespect me. I will pray for peace and understanding, in my own life and in the world at large.

 Pray

Almighty God, when I experience your presence within me in the person of Jesus, your Son, I experience hope and the promise of redemption, no matter how I might stumble. May that experience inspire me to treat others as Jesus would treat them, with patience and forgiveness. Amen.

Pray

"How shall I make a return to the Lord for all the good he has done for me? The cup of salvation I will take up, and I will call upon the name of the Lord." (Psalm 116:12-13)

 Read *John 13:1-15*

Summary: *"'I have given you a model to follow, so that as I have done for you, you should also do.'"* (John: 13:15)

Spend two minutes in silence. Then repeat this passage from Scripture, and let it speak to your heart.

Meditation

I read a homily in which the preacher reflected on how Jesus showed the depth of his love for humanity by setting aside his proper place as Lord and became instead the servant, setting an example for all of us.

In developing this theme, the preacher addressed his congregation and by implication all people by saying, "You are filthy and vile by nature and by deed. You are as spiritually disgusting as the nastiest, foulest pair of feet ever seen or smelt." He was referring to the fact that we all sin, repeatedly, and all need to be cleansed of our guilt.

But I don't think Jesus washed the feet of his apostles to emphasize how filthy human beings are, but rather to show now noble human beings can be.

Let us pray as we commemorate the Paschal Mystery that as he was a human being like us, we may be human beings like him.

Live Lent!

I will attend the Mass of the Lord's Supper and invite someone to join me.

Pray

Almighty God, the psalmist tells us that you made us a little lower than the angels and crowned us with glory and honor (Psalm 8:6). Through the ministry of Jesus, you taught us how noble humanity was made to be. May your Holy Spirit incline us to reject sin and to cultivate in our souls all that is good. Amen.

 ## Good Friday

 Pray

"Let your face shine upon your servant; save me in your kindness. . .. Take courage and be stouthearted, all you who hope in the Lord." (Psalm 31:17,25)

 Read *18:1-19:42*

Summary: *"When Jesus had taken the wine, he said, 'It is finished,' And bowing his head, he handed over the spirit." (John 19:30)*

Spend two minutes in silence. Then repeat this passage from Scripture, and let it speak to your heart.

Meditation

The crucifix is a distinctive feature of Catholic churches. In Christian churches of other denominations, it is more common to see a simple cross without the body of the crucified Jesus. The thinking behind the simple cross is that crucifixion was not the end of Jesus' life but the door, as it were, through which he passed from life on earth, where his divine nature was hidden, to life in heaven where the glory of the Son of God is fully revealed.

The crucifix that occupies a central place in a Catholic church, however, is meant to remind us that the sacrifice Jesus made on the cross on our behalf is present to us in the celebration of the Eucharist—not that it is just commemorated or reenacted but that it is literally present during every Mass.

This is important, because it keeps us aware of what Jesus endured in order to experience and defeat death so that we, too, can live with him forever; it is important also because it helps us to understand and accept that suffering is an inevitable part of human life.

May our participation in the sacrament of the Eucharist help us to see past our own hardships to the day when we will live at peace in the presence of God.

Live Lent!

I will attend the Good Friday liturgy, and I will invite someone to join me.

 Pray

Lord Jesus Christ, with faith in your love and mercy, I eat your flesh and drink your blood in the holy Eucharist. May the sacrament bring me, not condemnation, but rather health in spirit, mind, and body. Amen.

Holy Saturday

 Pray

"Give thanks to the Lord, for he is good, for his mercy endures forever." (Psalm 118:1)

 Read *Luke 24:1-12*

Summary: *"'Why do you seek the living one among the dead? He is not here, but he has been raised. Remember what he said to you while he was still in Galilee, that the Son of Man must be handed over to sinners and be crucified, and rise on the third day.'" (Luke 24:5b-7)*

Spend two minutes in silence. Then repeat this passage from Scripture, and let it speak to your heart.

Meditation

Why was the stone rolled back from the entrance to Jesus' tomb, as the author of Luke's Gospel describes in today's reading? Certainly, it wasn't to allow Jesus to leave the tomb—the same Jesus who in a few days would enter a room although the doors were locked.

The stone was moved so that the women who had come to the grave could see for themselves that Jesus was not there, and so that there could be no misunderstanding shortly thereafter when they met the risen Lord.

The testimony of those women as to what they had seen with their own eyes exploded with such power that it shook human history to its core.

May the reality of what those first disciples proclaimed continue to resound as an earthquake in our lives, filling us with gratitude for what God has done for us, and with faith in his promise of new life for all who love him.

Live Lent!

I will share with others the reason for my joy today. He is risen!

 Pray

Risen Lord, may the miracle of your resurrection, through which you overcame for humanity the consequences of both sin and death, always be for me a source of amazement and joy, and may I never waver in my gratitude for your gift of eternal life. Amen.

Pray

"The right hand of the Lord is exalted; the right hand of the Lord has struck with power. I shall not die, but live, and declare the works of the Lord." (Psalm 118:16-17)

 Read *John 20: 1-9*

Summary: *"Then the other disciple also went in, the one who had arrived at the tomb first, and he saw and believed."* (John 20:8)

Celebrate!

Share this table prayer with those you will eat with today.
Pray together:

> *Christ has risen! Alleluia!*
> *Loving God, you who create all things*
> *and generously give us all we need,*
> *we praise you and thank you for being present with us now*
> *as we celebrate the resurrection of Jesus Christ, your Son.*
>
> *Thank you for accompanying us on our Lenten journey;*
> *please be with us during this Easter season, and always,*
> *as we strive to live as disciples of your Son.*
>
> *May the breaking of bread, today and every day,*
> *remind us of the Bread of Life, Jesus Christ,*
> *who died to atone for our sins*
> *and rose again so that we, too, may rise*
> *and live in your presence forever.*
>
> *O God, bless this food and we who share it,*
> *and be with those who cannot share it with us.*

We ask this in the name of the same Jesus Christ, who lives and reigns with you and the Holy Spirit, one God, forever and ever. Amen.

Alleluia! Christ has risen!

APPENDIX

There are two solemnities and one feast that can fall during Lent. When they fall on Lenten weekdays, they are celebrated in place of the liturgy for those days. Meditations for these three days are included in this appendix. Check the liturgical calendar; in some jurisdictions, the dates on which these celebrations are held may be changed.

Feast of the Chair of Peter

FEBRUARY 22

 Pray

"Even though I walk in the dark valley I fear no evil; for you are at my side with your rod and your staff that give me courage." (Psalm 23:4)

 Read *Matthew 16:13-19*

Summary: *"'Who do people say that the Son of Man is?' They replied, 'Some say John the Baptist, others Elijah, still others Jeremiah or one of the prophets.' He said to them, 'But who do you say that I am?' Simon Peter said in reply, 'You are the Christ, the Son of the living God.'"* (Matthew 16:13b-16)

Spend two minutes in silence. Then repeat this passage from Scripture, and let it speak to your heart.

 Meditation

Visiting the Basilica of St. Peter in Rome, especially for the first time, can be overwhelming. The sheer size of the structure—one of the largest churches in the world—the vaulted ceilings, the soaring dome, and the multitude of altars and heroic monuments can be difficult to absorb. Soaring in the apse of the church is the extraordinary monument designed by Gian Lorenzo Bernini and completed in 1666. The centerpiece of this altar is a gilt bronze reliquary in the shape of a chair; within is an actual wooden chair, traditionally venerated as the chair used by Peter, the chief of the apostles and the first bishop of Rome. This chair consists of several parts, including some that may date to the ninth century.

The Church has set aside this day—even when it falls during Lent—in order to reflect on that chair, not as an important object in itself but as a symbol of the unity that Jesus wanted for his followers. That unity is grounded in our shared faith in Jesus as the Son of God and the savior of the world, in our mutual commitment to live in keeping with his Gospel of love, and our identification with each other as members of his body, the Church. Whenever we sin, either by an overt act or by neglect, we harm the Body of Christ and undermine the unity Jesus prayed for. By contrast, as we refresh our relationship with God during Lent, we contribute new vitality to the life of the whole Church.

Live Lent!

Today, I will pray the Nicene Creed, reflecting after each phrase how my faith in the teachings of the Church unite me with Catholic men and women around the world and across time.

 Pray

Lord Jesus Christ, you prayed that your followers might be one as you and the Father are one. May I be an instrument of the unity you desire by remaining faithful to your Gospel and by witnessing to it through a life of service to others. Amen.

Solemnity of St. Joseph, Husband of Mary

MARCH 19

 Pray

"The promises of the LORD I will sing forever; through all generations my mouth shall proclaim your faithfulness, For you have said, 'My kindness is established forever'; in heaven you have confirmed your faithfulness." (Psalm 89:2-3)

Read *Matthew 1:16; 18-21; 24a*

Summary: *"When Joseph awoke, he did as the angel of the Lord had commanded him and took his wife into his home." (Matthew 1:24)*

Spend two minutes in silence. Then repeat this passage from Scripture, and let it speak to your heart.

Meditation

One characteristic of the Scriptures that frustrates many readers is that the authors provide so few details about most of the personalities they write about. In the Gospels, for instance, many would like to know more about the magi, Simeon and Anna, the individual apostles, Lazarus, or the wife of Pontius Pilate. And certainly, many would like to know more about Joseph, the husband of Mary.

The solemnity we celebrate today, even during Lent, indicates the esteem in which the Church holds Joseph. But the Gospel of Mark doesn't mention him at all and the Gospel of John mentions him only in passing. We never hear him speak. All we know about him is contained in relatively few passages in the Gospels of Matthew and Luke, and we know nothing of him from the time Jesus was 12 years old.

But the evangelists were not writing biography in the modern sense of the word; they were writing the story of our salvation. They told us about Joseph only what they thought we needed to know. What we need to know is that Joseph was a devout man who observed the Law of God; that he was a just man whose only goal was to shield Mary from opprobrium when he learned that she was pregnant; that he was a faithful man who submitted to what he understood to be God's will; and that he was a courageous and responsible man who took care of his family under the most difficult circumstances.

We know enough to see Joseph as our model and to do our best to imitate his qualities, keeping faith with God as we navigate the twists and turns in our own lives.

Live Lent!

I will spend time reflecting on decisions I make in everyday life and major decisions I may have to make in the foreseeable future. I will ask the Holy Spirit to help me understand God's will before I make any significant choice.

 Pray

Almighty God, you chose Joseph as the guardian of Jesus and his mother, Mary. Help me, like Joseph, to always see clearly the role you have chosen for me and to carry it out according to your will. Amen.

Solemnity of the Annunciation of the Lord

MARCH 25

 Pray

"To do your will, O my God, is my delight, and your law is within my heart." (Psalm 40:9)

 Read *Luke 1:26-38*

Summary: *"You shall conceive and bear a son and give him the name Jesus. Great will be his dignity and he will be called the Son of the Most High."* (Luke 1:31-32)

Spend two minutes in silence. Then repeat this passage from Scripture, and let it speak to your heart.

 Meditation

I grew up in the 1940s and 1950s when everyday conversation wasn't nearly as candid as it is now.

For example, many people wouldn't say the word "pregnant," using a euphemism such as "expecting" instead. When Lucille Ball became pregnant with her second child in 1952, the pregnancy was written into the story line of "I Love Lucy," but CBS wouldn't let the actors use the word "pregnant."

Well, when we celebrate the solemnity that interrupts the sober mood of Lent today, we don't pull any punches. This celebration is about the fact that Mary was pregnant. The Church makes that clear by placing this observance on March 25—nine months before Christmas.

Mary was pregnant, and she was going to experience the growth of the child within her and give birth to him—a human being who came into the world as a human being does.

Jesus, the son she conceived and carried and gave birth to, would experience everything it is to be a human being—except sin. He would grow. He would study and learn. He would work. He would embark on a ministry that thrilled and comforted some and irritated and alienated others.

He would suffer, and he would die, and he would disappear from view—as every human being does. It was no illusion. Jesus, Mary's son, was a human being. But he was also the Divine Being, the Second Person of the Trinity, God—and death could not contain him, as we will celebrate in two weeks, and because of his sacrifice and triumph, neither can death contain us.

Live Lent!

I will pray in thanksgiving that God really took on human form and became one of us, so that we might be freed from the power of sin and death and live in his company forever.

 Pray

Almighty God, you came into the world in human form to overcome for us the consequences of sin and death. May we live in a way that shows our gratitude for your Son's sacrifice on our behalf, and may we die with confidence in the power of the resurrection. Amen.

ABOUT THE AUTHORS

Sr. Theresa Rickard, OP, President and Executive Director of RENEW International, is a Dominican Sister of Blauvelt, New York. She holds the degree of Doctor of Ministry in Preaching from Aquinas Institute of Theology in St. Louis, Missouri. Additionally, she earned the degree of Master of Divinity from Union Theological Seminary in New York City and the degree of Master of Arts in Religion and Religious Education from Fordham University, New York City.

Sr. Terry is a national speaker, preacher, and author. She has written two Advent and Lent devotionals in the *Living Gospel* series published by Ave Maria Press. She is also a contributing author to *Preaching in the Sunday Assembly* and *We Preach Christ Crucified*, published by Liturgical Press. Sr. Terry is a regular contributor to the RENEW International blog under the title "God in the Stuff of Life," and you can follower her on Twitter at @SrTerryRickard.

Before joining the RENEW staff, she ministered in two parishes in the South Bronx and was the Director of Vocation and Formation Ministry for her Dominican congregation. She also was a member of the Archdiocese of New York Parish Mission Team.

Charles Paolino, a graduate of Seton Hall University and the Pennsylvania State University, is managing editor at RENEW International and a permanent deacon of the Diocese of Metuchen. He has written two Lenten devotionals and an Advent devotional in the *Living Gospel* series published by Ave Maria Press and is a columnist for *The Catholic Spirit*, the newspaper of the Diocese of Metuchen. His work has also appeared in *L'Osservatore Romano*.

Presenting RENEW International

The RENEW process, both parish-based and diocese-wide, was developed and implemented in the Archdiocese of Newark, New Jersey. Its success there led other dioceses to bring RENEW to their people in over 160 dioceses in the United States and 24 countries.

Over four decades, RENEW International has grown from its original single RENEW process. Materials and training have been inculturated and made available in more than 40 languages. We have added specific pastoral outreach to campuses and to young adults in their 20s and 30s. We have incorporated prison ministry and provided resources for the visually impaired.

The core of all these processes remains the same: to help people become better hearers and doers of the Word of God. We do this by encouraging and supporting the formation of small communities that gather prayerfully to reflect on and share the Word of God, to make better connections between faith and life, and to live their faith more concretely in family, work, and community life.

As a not-for-profit organization, we sustain our pastoral outreach in part from the sales of our publications and resources and stipends for services we provide to parishes and dioceses. However, our priority is always to serve all parishes that desire to renew their faith and build the Church, regardless of their economic situation. We have been able to fulfill this mission not only in the inner- city and rural areas of the United States, but also in the developing world, especially Latin America and Africa, thanks to donations and charitable funding.

As you meet in your small group, we invite you to take a few moments to imagine the great invisible network of others, here in the United States and on other continents. They gather, as you do, in small Christian communities, around the Word of God present in the Scripture, striving to hear and act upon that Word. Keep them in your prayer: a prayer of thanksgiving for the many graces we have experienced; a prayer that the Holy Spirit will guide all of us as we Live Lent!

The Structure and Flow of a Session

A faith-sharing session typically lasts about 90 minutes. The following outline for your weekly small-group meeting suggests how your time might be allocated in order to keep the group moving smoothly from one element to the next. The time frame described here is based on the assumption that participants have read the session beforehand and considered their responses to the sharing questions, making notes in the spaces provided. Of course, the group leader may adjust the timing according to the dynamics of a particular session.

More detailed suggestions for the leader are included in *Essentials for Small Group Leaders* and *Leading Prayer in Small Groups,* both available from RENEW International. For details, visit www.renewintl.org.

Introductions · 5 minutes

If the group has not met before, if participants do not know each other, or if someone new has joined, an opportunity to get acquainted is important. People share most easily when they feel comfortable and accepted in a group.

Focus · 5 minutes

Read the focus to call to mind the central theme of the session.

Opening Song · 5 minutes

Play a song recommended for the session or a song of your own choosing.

Opening Prayer · 5 minutes

A few moments of silence should precede the prayer, which is always at the heart of gatherings of Christians.

Gospel Reading and Reflection · 20 minutes

A member of the group proclaims the Gospel. After a few minutes of silent reflection, the leader asks if anyone would like to share on the passage.

Old Testament Connection and Reflection • 20 minutes

Members of the group take a few minutes to review the Old Testament Connection, or a member of the group may read it aloud; then those who wish share their responses to the question. This section is not a discussion of the Old Testament reading for the day's Mass, but rather a reflection on the background in Hebrew Scriptures for the Gospel reading of the day.

Meditation • 25 minutes

Members of the group take a few minutes to review the Meditation, or a member of the group may read it aloud. Members review or consider their answers to the questions; then they share their responses to one or more of the questions.

Closing Prayer • 5 minutes

Note on the music

Songs are suggested for the moments of prayer at the opening of each small-group Sunday session. Music selections for Live Lent! are provided by our partners at OCP. The music is available as individual songs or as a nine-song digital album or "virtual CD." The individual songs and the digital album are available for purchase through RENEW International at ocp.org/renew-music.

from RENEW International

Live Lent! Year A, B, C

Continue your Lenten journey with the other titles in this series for lectionary years B and C.

All three titles are written by RENEW's own Sister Terry Rickard. *Live Lent!* will help you make the most of this season of preparation and spiritual renewal.

- Gather weekly in small groups
- Get inspired by the Sunday Gospel readings
- Explore Old Testament insights
- Reflect and pray **each day of the week**
- Take action in everyday life

Advent Awakenings

Advent is a time of spiritual anticipation amidst the often distracting preparations for Christmas. Stay focused on the significance of this season with *Advent Awakenings*, a four-session faith-sharing experience grounded in the Sunday gospel readings.

The *Advent Awakening* series is based on the three-year cycle of the Lectionary. Each book contains four sessions corresponding with the four Sundays of Advent and presents themes drawn from the Sunday gospel readings, plus enriching devotions for family use. Appropriate for seasonal groups, small Christian communities, and individual reflection and prayer.

Year B: Take the Time: Encourages participants to prepare for Jesus' coming by setting aside everyday busyness and become more deeply aware of God's beckoning.

Year A: Trust the Lord: Urges participants to have confidence that God's challenging call is the true way to prepare for union with Christ.

Year C: Say Yes to God: Prompts participants to accept the invitation of Jesus' coming by reflecting on how to be more open to his presence in their lives.

Also available as an eBook!

For more information visit www.renewintl.org/seasonal

RENEW Small-Group Leader Series

Essentials for Small-Group Leaders

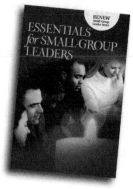

This book offers a comprehensive collection of pastoral insights and practical suggestions to help small community leaders guide their groups in a way that nourishes spiritual growth. Culled from RENEW International's almost four decades of experience in pioneering and promoting small Christian communities, this book overflows with simple but effective ideas and strategies that will enhance the way these groups reflect on and respond to the Gospel.

Leading Prayer in Small Groups

Have you ever been asked to lead prayer for your church group, council,

or committee? RENEW International has developed a helpful resource called Leading Prayer in Small Groups to encourage you in leading fruitful group prayer experiences with confidence. *Leading Prayer in Small Groups* emphasizes the importance of group prayer for church groups of every kind and provides insight into why we pray. It also explains the role, qualities, and duties of a leader of prayer. Readers are guided through the stages of preparing group prayer and the process of effectively leading prayer for a group.

Visit www.renewintl.org/leaders to learn more or to order.

Spirituality for Everyday Life
with Ronald Rolheiser

Based on best-selling author Ronald Rolheiser, OMI's books *The Shattered Lantern, The Holy Longing,* and *Sacred Fire,* the *Spirituality for Everyday Life* with Ronald Rolheiser Series explores the phases of discipleship and how to live as Christ's disciples in today's world.

Longing for the Holy

Longing for the Holy is for those who want to enrich their sense of the presence of God. Designed for either a small group faith-sharing experience

or personal reflection, participants explore the implications of the central mysteries of faith—the Incarnation, the Eucharist, and the Paschal Mystery —for spirituality. Attending to the cultural challenges that keep us from realizing our true desire, it considers the important themes of church community, justice, sexuality, the practices of the spiritual life, and being a mystic of the everyday.

Living in the Sacred

Living in the Sacred is a follow-up faith-sharing resource for *Longing for the Holy* and is based on Ronald Rolheiser's, *Sacred Fire. Living in the Sacred* takes participants on a deeper spiritual journey exploring the second stage of discipleship: "Giving your life away". Having moved through the "getting your life together" stage participants have made life commitments either in marriage or other relationships, child raising, to sick or elderly parents or other relatives, careers, communities, etc. *Living in the Sacred* is about how we stay true to these commitments as disciples of Christ.

For more information visit www.renewintl.org/spirituality

Connect with us!

Now it's easier than ever to connect with the RENEW International community for daily spiritual insights and updates.

 www.facebook.com/RENEWIntl

 blog.renewintl.org

 @RENEWIntl

 YouTube.com/user/RENEWInternational